THE MESSAGE

of

LEADERSHIP

THE MESSAGE TEXT BY EUGENE H. PETERSON

—

THE MESSAGE

of

LEADERSHIP

31 ESSENTIAL INSIGHTS
from PROVERBS

—

DEVOTIONAL TEXT BY DANIEL SOUTHERN

NAVPRESS®

BRINGING TRUTH TO LIFE

OUR GUARANTEE TO YOU

We believe so strongly in the message of our books that we are making this quality guarantee to you. If for any reason you are disappointed with the content of this book, return the title page to us with your name and address and we will refund to you the list price of the book. To help us serve you better, please briefly describe why you were disappointed. Mail your refund request to: NavPress, P.O. Box 35002, Colorado Springs, CO 80935.

The Navigators is an international Christian organization. Our mission is to advance the gospel of Jesus and His kingdom into the nations through spiritual generations of laborers living and discipling among the lost. We see a vital movement of the gospel, fueled by prevailing prayer, flowing freely through relational networks and out into the nations where workers for the kingdom are next door to everywhere.

NavPress is the publishing ministry of The Navigators. The mission of NavPress is to reach, disciple, and equip people to know Christ and make Him known by publishing life-related materials that are biblically rooted and culturally relevant. Our vision is to stimulate spiritual transformation through every product we publish.

ISBN 1-60006-085-4
ISBN 13 9-78160006-085-4

Cover design by Studiogearbox.com
Cover image by John Knill / Digital Vision
Creative Team: Kent Wilson, Lori Mitchell, John Blase, Darla Hightower, Arvid Wallen, Bob Bubnis

Some of the anecdotal illustrations in this book are true to life and are included with the permission of the persons involved. All other illustrations are composites of real situations, and any resemblance to people living or dead is coincidental.

Published in association with the literary agency of Alive Communications, Inc., 7680 Goddard Street, Suite 200, Colorado Springs, CO 80920 (www.alivecommunications.com).

Printed in the United States of America

2 3 4 5 6 7 8 / 11 10 09 08 07

FOR A FREE CATALOG OF NAVPRESS BOOKS & BIBLE STUDIES,
CALL 1-800-366-7788 (USA) OR 1-800-839-4769 (CANADA).

DEDICATION

This devotional is dedicated to those who have patiently taught me over a lifetime through loving relationships. To my mother, Elizabeth; my father, Robert; my brother, Phil; my son, Adam; my daughter, Tyler; and most of all to my wife, Lori without whom I could not hope to accomplish anything worthwhile. Lori, you are the bedrock of my life.

I also want to acknowledge those who have mentored me over the years including my Uncle Wayne Cummins, John Dillon, Sterling Huston, Charlie Riggs, and Charles Ryrie. Thank you for investing in my life so unselfishly.

Thank you each one,
Daniel Southern

Contents

Introduction

This work is intended for those who lead others or aspire to do so. There are all kinds of leaders. I am six foot six and a former college athlete, so simply by virtue of my physical stature I have often been thrust into a leadership role. But leadership is not found in our physical prowess, as the diminutive Napoleon could well attest. Neither is leadership found in our social standing or our intelligence, although all of these things can lend themselves to effective leadership.

Leadership springs from within us and is difficult to fully explain. It is almost easier to define leadership by what it is not, than by what it is. Leaders are *not* passive, they do *not* give up easily, and they are *not* easily intimidated by circumstances. In untying some of the "nots" of leadership, I have come to believe that leadership *is* primarily a state of mind.

You may not think of yourself as a leader — I never did. I only knew that when there was something that needed to be done, I didn't want to wait for someone else to step up to the plate. Leaders can be selfish, egotistical, empire builders or they can be servants, initiators, and problem solvers. Maybe leaders are a little bit of all of the above — and more. It is up to each one of us to choose what kind of leader we want to be.

I have been blessed by a variety of experiences that have shaped my understanding of leadership. I have met presidents and I have lunched with the homeless in a soup kitchen. I have traveled the world and I have coached little league football in our hometown. I have led large enterprises and I have stacked chairs after a church service. I'll draw upon all of these experiences as I attempt to unfold for you the lessons I've learned.

While leadership may resist tight definition, I believe we have been given guidance along leadership's path; this guidance is found in the ancient Proverbs. My initiation into leadership started over three decades ago when I went to work for Billy Graham. After almost twenty years with Billy Graham, I again find myself being initiated into yet another aspect of leadership. Over the past decade I have led an historic Christian ministry that focuses on unpacking the Christian message so it is accessible to anyone interested in finding God. At the American Tract Society (www.ATStracts.org) we have been developing resources for over 180 years so everyone can understand the Christian gospel. Our challenge today is to do this in an effective and relevant manner.

I am not sure what will be next, but I do know that my life's purpose and energies must continue to be more focused toward getting to know God better each day and helping others do the same thing.

The marketplace is filled with books on leadership. I have held off on this writing project for a long time because I wanted to write something that made a genuine contribution to the reader's life; something not easily set aside after the first reading, but turned to over and over again as a valuable tool. This little resource is an attempt to have a ministry like that in your life.

My approach will be to give you a portion of Proverbs and a practical insight for each day of the month. My hope is that this will prompt you to think more deeply about God's working in your life as a leader. One of the most beneficial disciplines I have picked up through the years has been to read and reread the ancient wisdom of Proverbs. Because there are thirty-one chapters, it is tailor-made for reading a chapter a day for a month and then starting over again to gain ever greater understanding of its teachings month after month and year after year.

I pray that this resource will speak to your heart each time you open its pages.

Daniel Southern

For a companion Bible study to this book go to www.DanielSouthern.com.

I Walk Before You Run

Gentlemen, this is a football.
— VINCE LOMBARDI

PROVERBS 1:1-9

These are the wise sayings of Solomon,
    David's son, Israel's king —
Written down so we'll know how to live well and right,
    to understand what life means and where it's going;
A manual for living,
    for learning what's right and just and fair;
To teach the inexperienced the ropes
    and give our young people a grasp on reality.
There's something here also for seasoned men and women,
    still a thing or two for the experienced to learn —
Fresh wisdom to probe and penetrate,
    the rhymes and reasons of wise men and women.
Start with GOD — the first step in learning is bowing down to GOD;
    only fools thumb their noses at such wisdom and learning.
Pay close attention, friend, to what your father tells you;
    never forget what you learned at your mother's knee.
Wear their counsel like flowers in your hair,
    like rings on your fingers.

Coach Vince Lombardi was well known for keeping his team focused on the fundamentals of the game. How about you? Are you crystal clear about the fundamentals of the game of life? Do you even know what game you are playing? In reality, of course, life is no game; it is the most serious business in which you will ever engage. And since this is not a dress rehearsal, strive to do it right and start with the fundamentals.

The writer of Proverbs starts with the foundational concept that wisdom is the chief aim of life and goes on to say that all wisdom comes from God. If you put God first everything else will fall into place.

How do you do this? It starts with humbling yourself and admitting that God is the coach and you are the player. He calls the plays and you execute them — sometimes over and over again, always learning more about God and yourself. And you keep at it, always reminding yourself that the coach has a perspective of the game you'll never have.

The legendary coach Tom Landry once told me that he had three priorities in life: God, family, and football — in that order. "Until you get your priorities straight you will never be truly successful at anything."

Life is not a game; it is serious business and the stakes are eternally high. You must start with the fundamentals. Gentlemen, there is a God and we're not Him!

ESSENTIAL INSIGHT 1: *Start with the fundamentals and stick with them.*

2　Little Things Add Up

Knowledge is power.
(Ipsa Scientia Potestas Est)
— SIR FRANCIS BACON

PROVERBS 2:1-5

Good friend, take to heart what I'm telling you;
　　collect my counsels and guard them with your life.
Tune your ears to the world of Wisdom;
　　set your heart on a life of Understanding.
That's right — if you make Insight your priority,
　　and won't take no for an answer,
Searching for it like a prospector panning for gold,
　　like an adventurer on a treasure hunt,
Believe me, before you know it Fear-of-GOD will be yours;
　　you'll have come upon the Knowledge of God.

Rome — the very name evokes images of empires and an atmosphere of greatness. One of her generals, Quintus Sertorius, found himself far from home in Spain with a vast territory to defend and an army composed almost entirely of undisciplined conscripts. He had no interest in defeat, so he called them together to teach them an important lesson on what it would take to be a successful army.

He brought out the most physically impressive warrior in his ranks and also the smallest and least conspicuous soldier. In front of the great warrior he placed a small scraggly pony and in front of the smaller soldier he placed a mighty war horse. He then gave each the task of pulling out the horse's tail, but by two very different methods. The stout soldier was instructed to pull off the tail in one clump while the small soldier was told to do so one hair at a time. You can guess the outcome. It was the weaker soldier who triumphed over the war horse and the mighty soldier who failed despite all his apparent advantages. A horse's tail is strong because of its many strands.

A wise leader will succeed by attending to the many seemingly small principles for life's success offered by God. These principles will be like the multitude of strands on the horse's tail making it impervious to being overpowered by brute force. A foolish person relies on individual gifts and personal strength; however, this is the epitome of weakness, because there is no unity of purpose supporting his efforts. Therefore, he stands alone. Leadership finds its strength by pulling together the many hairs of the horse's tail.

ESSENTIAL INSIGHT 2: *Don't look merely to your natural gifts, but focus your energy on marshalling all available resources.*

3   Who's on First?

My religion consists of a humble admiration of the illimitable superior spirit
who reveals himself in the slight details we are able to perceive with our frail
and feeble mind.

— ALBERT EINSTEIN

PROVERBS 3:5-10

Trust GOD from the bottom of your heart;
  don't try to figure out everything on your own.
Listen for GOD's voice in everything you do, everywhere you go;
  he's the one who will keep you on track.
Don't assume that you know it all.
  Run to GOD! Run from evil!
Your body will glow with health,
  your very bones will vibrate with life!
Honor GOD with everything you own;
  give him the first and the best.
Your barns will burst,
  your wine vats will brim over.

Who has first place in your life? Your job? Your favorite pastime? Money? Leisure? What is at the top?

As a young man, I often put my foot in my mouth. I will never forget walking out across a vast stadium filled with people, leading Billy Graham to his pulpit at the start of one of his campaigns in a foreign country. The police officer assigned to escort Mr. Graham was accompanying us, and in a burst of enthusiasm I said to the officer, "If you're not careful, we might make you into a Protestant." Billy turned to the man with a gentle smile and said, "No, we won't do that. But I hope we will help you to find God."

Have you found God? He has been searching for you all your life. You must remember, though, that God is a gentleman and won't barge in. You have to invite Him in. And there is a second step in all relationships — that is to get to an intimacy and friendship beyond the superficial level. Do you have an intimacy with God? One that allows you to trust Him to look out for your best interests so you don't have to?

Granted, we all struggle with establishing priorities and sticking to them. But have you ever articulated the priority that you want God to be in your life? The wisdom of Proverbs indicates that if God is at the top, every other aspect of life will fall into place. I have put this promise to the test in my own life and can vouch for its reliability. God always keeps His word. We will fail, but He never fails.

ESSENTIAL INSIGHT 3: *Decide to put God ahead of everything else in your life.*

4 The Heart of the Matter

The happiness of a man in this life does not consist in the absence but in the mastery of his passions.
— ALFRED LORD TENNYSON

PROVERBS 4:23-27

Keep vigilant watch over your heart;
  that's where life starts.
Don't talk out of both sides of your mouth;
  avoid careless banter, white lies, and gossip.
Keep your eyes straight ahead;
  ignore all sideshow distractions.
Watch your step,
  and the road will stretch out smooth before you.
Look neither right nor left;
  leave evil in the dust.

The Western world considers the heart as the seat of our emotions; however, this is not necessarily so in other cultures. For example, in Africa it is the liver. So in Africa you would not say, "still your heart," but rather, "don't let your liver quiver." It's not the words but the meaning that the writer of Proverbs wanted to get across in chapter 4. Guard your heart!

Your emotions are a powerful force. Do you control them or do they control you? Your passions can be the source of much evil. At the same time, great good can be accomplished if your heart's focus is properly directed.

God has given a set of perfect and reliable guidelines in His Word that will direct our lives if we place our passions under their authority. But it requires a practiced decision we must make in theory, well ahead of the practical test. Moral spontaneity is the breeding ground of ethical failure. Prayer can play an important role in helping us to predetermine our behavior as we face the challenges of life.

We contain our emotions through our will and intellect if we are wise. This is accomplished by thinking through our values and priorities before the adrenaline starts to pump. Many a high school date has taken a turn toward unwise promiscuity because behavior had not been considered before the windows got steamed up.

I have seen leaders lose their reputation and moral authority in the snap of the finger — something I have done myself. You can destroy something you have built up over a long time in a matter of seconds if you let your passions get the better of you.

ESSENTIAL INSIGHT 4: *Give your heart to God and channel your passions toward personal growth.*

5 Standing on Home Plate

The most important persuasion tool you have in your entire arsenal is integrity.
— ZIG ZIGLAR

PROVERBS 5:21-22
Mark well that GOD doesn't miss a move you make;
   he's aware of every step you take.
The shadow of your sin will overtake you;
   you'll find yourself stumbling all over yourself in the dark.

A famous Christian couple invited me to be a guest on their television show several years ago. Toward the end of my visit, I was told that one very attractive staff woman was the former wife of another staff member on the program, who was now sporting a new wife. I was very disturbed by the nonchalant manner in which this had been shared with me — as if it were no big deal. Months later we all discovered this was only the tip of the iceberg as news came out of the fall of Jim and Tammy Faye Bakker's *PTL Club*.

What a person does in his private life is a strong indication of what is going on in his heart. And what could be more private than the sexual relationship you have with your spouse? If a leader is unfaithful to his spouse, he is unfaithful to all who would follow him. This is so because the marriage relationship is the foundation for all other relationships we form in society and it mirrors our character.

Marriage is a promise that puts someone else's interests ahead of your own. Leadership, like marriage, is as much a responsibility as it is a privilege and is based on trust earned over time through hard work. If a follower cannot trust you, will they follow you?

ESSENTIAL INSIGHT 5: *Integrity starts at home. Learn to be a person of your word and stick with your commitments even when you no longer feel like it.*

6 Flat Tire on the Fast Track

He that can have patience can have what he will.
— BENJAMIN FRANKLIN

PROVERBS 6:1-5

Dear friend, if you've gone into hock with your neighbor
    or locked yourself into a deal with a stranger,
If you've impulsively promised the shirt off your back
    and now find yourself shivering out in the cold,
Friend, don't waste a minute, get yourself out of that mess.
    You're in that man's clutches!
    Go, put on a long face; act desperate.
Don't procrastinate —
    there's no time to lose.
Run like a deer from the hunter,
    fly like a bird from the trapper!

An acquaintance of mine bought one of the first DeLoreans to come off the assembly line. You have probably heard the story of DeLorean's amazing rise to success in the auto industry with development of the Ford GTO and then later his own car make named after himself. But he lost it all — his family, his business, and yes, even his car — because he went too far too fast in his pursuit of success. Patience was not a virtue in the fast-paced auto industry in which the young and ambitious DeLorean circulated.

What you may not know is that John DeLorean became a follower of Christ when he hit the speed bumps of life. He reinvented himself. I think it's safe to say that DeLorean learned the truth of Proverbs 6:1-5 late in life after he had almost given himself away to his debtors and strangers while traveling the fast track in search of fame and success.

It is never too late to throw on the brakes if you detect that you are on the wrong road. Be honest with yourself and ask God to help you develop the patience you need to wait on Him and not create your own success. When you see a door of opportunity, there is nothing wrong with turning the door's handle to see if it will open, but heartache can follow if you break down a door that is locked. Creating my own success also places a burden on me to sustain that which I have created. On the other hand, when God allows me to go through a door, it is He who keeps the door open, and I can rest in that partnership.

ESSENTIAL INSIGHT 6: *Patiently wait on God for your success, and He will give you results greater than you could engineer on your own.*

7 She'll Steal Your Heart

I can think of nothing less pleasurable than a life devoted to pleasure.
— JOHN D. ROCKEFELLER

PROVERBS 7:4-10

Talk to Wisdom as to a sister.
    Treat Insight as your companion.
They'll be with you to fend off the Temptress —
    that smooth-talking, honey-tongued Seductress.
As I stood at the window of my house
    looking out through the shutters,
Watching the mindless crowd stroll by,
    I spotted a young man without any sense
Arriving at the corner of the street where she lived,
    then turning up the path to her house.
It was dusk, the evening coming on,
    the darkness thickening into night.
Just then, a woman met him —
    she'd been lying in wait for him, dressed to seduce him.

Proverbs references illicit sex and loose women more than any other single subject. The writer certainly thinks this is an important topic for us to consider. But the message goes far deeper than one might think.

Anything that ignites your desires and passions to the detriment of your good judgment and common sense could be considered a harlot who would potentially steal your heart and fracture your life.

Who or what is the harlot that wants to steal your life? What is it that has the potential to bring you to ruin if you give in to its unhealthy attraction? It might be some form of addiction, sex, the lust for power or influence — maybe it is ambition. It is seen time and again in the lives of famous men and women consumed by some uncontrolled appetite.

Years ago I met one such flame that burned out too early; his name was Roger Miller. Backstage in Wheeling, West Virginia, Roger was about to go on stage for a performance. He was drunk and smoking like a house on fire. Roger was a man of great musical talent and humor — a gifted individual, but just a few short years later he was dead of cancer at the age of fifty-six. His untimely death appeared to have been hastened by his bad habits and a fast life lived on the road. What a waste! All the talent in the world could not overcome the harlot of hard living and reckless pursuit of pleasure.

If you have a clear mission in life, you will not be easily distracted by the sideshows along the way.

ESSENTIAL INSIGHT 7: *Focus your life on a meaningful mission that inspires your personal discipline and single-mindedness. Don't give in to your unseemly passions.*

8 The Street Where You Live

It is our choices . . . that show what we truly are, far more than our abilities.
— J. K. ROWLING

PROVERBS 8:12-16

"I am Lady Wisdom, and I live next to Sanity;
    Knowledge and Discretion live just down the street.
The Fear-of-GOD means hating Evil,
    whose ways I hate with a passion —
    pride and arrogance and crooked talk.
Good counsel and common sense are my characteristics;
    I am both Insight and the Virtue to live it out.
With my help, leaders rule,
    and lawmakers legislate fairly;
With my help, governors govern,
    along with all in legitimate authority."

Y ou have a choice as to the street where you live. You choose not only your home but those who will live next door. Your choices affect your relationship with God and the outcome of everything you do.

In the coffee shop of the Atlanta airport, Heavyweight Boxing Champion of the World Ken Norton sent an autograph seeker away with a terse remark — "Get out of here, can't you see I am eating!" The dejected sailor turned and walked away from his hero and straight toward me. I felt compassion for the navy seaman dressed in his white uniform, so I tried to encourage him. As we talked over a cup of coffee, he opened up and our conversation went quickly to a much deeper level than either of us had expected. Soon we were talking about eternity, and he was giving his life to Jesus as his personal Savior.

That seaman had started out seeking his hero's autograph and meeting disappointment; he ended up talking to someone just as ordinary as he was but meeting his Maker.

I was unimpressed with the boxer that day and pleasantly surprised by the sailor. In the eyes of many, the boxer had made all the right moves, but I saw something else. I was looking at a man whose choices had given him a black eye — at least in the mind of two people I knew. He had gone for fortune, fame, and money and lost his compassion for others.

Choices — we all make them every day. But in the end, they make us.

ESSENTIAL INSIGHT 8: *Choose to cultivate your inner person, and don't sacrifice your character on the road to success.*

9 What Are You Here For?

To forget one's purpose is the commonest form of stupidity.
— FRIEDRICH NIETZSCHE

PROVERBS 9:3-6

Having dismissed her serving maids,
    Lady Wisdom goes to town, stands in a prominent place,
    and invites everyone within sound of her voice:
"Are you confused about life, don't know what's going on?
    Come with me, oh come, have dinner with me!
I've prepared a wonderful spread — fresh-baked bread,
    roast lamb, carefully selected wines.
Leave your impoverished confusion and *live*!
    Walk up the street to a life with meaning."

We do not all have the same abilities or opportunities. But we do all have the privilege of deciding the purpose to which we will dedicate ourselves. A wise man once told me that there were only three big decisions that most of us will ever make in life: who we are going to live our lives with; what we are going to live our lives in; and what we are going to live our lives for. It's that third decision that seems to stump most of us. What are you living your life for?

As a college student, I worked for a time in an automotive plant to fund my schooling. It was a monotonous, routine job that I found unfulfilling. Most of my coworkers hated their jobs too and talked about how they would live out their retirement doing what they really wanted to do. Unfortunately, most folks never live out their dreams in retirement, and more importantly, why should we wait? I determined right then and there that I would ask God to help me find a purpose in my life that I could live for each day. I wanted something that made me wake up every morning and thank God for letting me be alive.

Have you found a worthwhile purpose in your life? Success has been defined as "the progressive realization of a worthwhile, predetermined goal." Establish a handful of worthy goals in your life and give yourself fully to accomplishing them. In establishing your life purposes, start with your relationship with God, your family, and your work. These top three areas of your life need the most urgent attention.

ESSENTIAL INSIGHT 9: *Settle on your life purposes and set out to accomplish them each day.*

10 It Will Wreck Your Life

*Confidence . . . thrives on honesty, on honor, on the sacredness of obligations,
on faithful protection and on unselfish performance.*
— FRANKLIN D. ROOSEVELT

PROVERBS 10:1-7
Wise son, glad father;
    stupid son, sad mother.
Ill-gotten gain gets you nowhere;
    an honest life is immortal.
GOD won't starve an honest soul,
    but he frustrates the appetites of the wicked.
Sloth makes you poor;
    diligence brings wealth.
Make hay while the sun shines — that's smart;
    go fishing during harvest — that's stupid.
Blessings accrue on a good and honest life,
    but the mouth of the wicked is a dark cave of abuse.
A good and honest life is a blessed memorial;
    a wicked life leaves a rotten stench.

A dishonest life is full of rot and will be exposed, causing you great embarrassment. It is not a question of "if" but "when" you will be exposed. The writer of Proverbs exalts the virtue of honesty. Where does honesty rank in your set of values? I am ashamed to admit that I have often struggled with being honest. Maybe you have failings in this area of your life too.

Years ago, I learned a very important lesson about verbal honesty that is seared on my consciousness. I hope it will help you as it has helped me. A friend of mine wanted to come visit me for the weekend but had responsibilities at his church that needed his attention. In order to get permission to leave, he told the entire congregation that I had been hurt in a car accident and he was needed at my bedside. Someone in the audience knew a girl I was dating and found out that my friend was lying — what an embarrassment when the truth leaked out!

The theory of six degrees of separation says that no one is more than six relationships removed from anyone else. This idea is not just about networking — it speaks to your need to be honest as well. Once you are proven to be dishonest, it is difficult to regain the trust of others; difficult, but not impossible. Confess your lie immediately or take back what was stolen. Don't let it go uncorrected or it will fester and become a "rotten stench" in your character. Face up to your sin and admit that it is wrong. That is the pathway to healing and restoration. There is nothing so pure and strong as a man with a clear conscience.

ESSENTIAL INSIGHT 10: *Determine that honesty will be a hallmark of your life and pay scrupulous attention to maintaining it at all times, no matter what the cost.*

II   Getting What You Need

Generosity is not giving me that which I need more than you do, but it is giving me that which you need more than I do.

— KAHLIL GIBRAN

PROVERBS 11:24-26

The world of the generous gets larger and larger;
  the world of the stingy gets smaller and smaller.
The one who blesses others is abundantly blessed;
  those who help others are helped.
Curses on those who drive a hard bargain!
  Blessings on all who play fair and square!

King Midas was the epitome of greed. You remember the story. He wished that everything he touched would turn to gold. He got his wish but eventually ruined his own happiness when he accidentally turned his daughter into a golden statue. He got what he wanted but lost what he needed.

I have always struggled with a desire to keep everything for myself. Maybe it has to do with being a spoiled first-born child. Maybe it is just a part of my selfish, sinful nature. I am blessed beyond measure to be married to one of the most giving people I have ever met. My wife, Lori, is always giving away more than I think she should. As you could imagine, this difference has caused friction in our marriage from time to time. One day I pondered my wife's "over-exuberance" in giving, and the Lord seemed to speak directly to my heart. I was reminded that she has a special gift in an area where I am weak. Instead of squelching that gift, I should be celebrating God's generosity toward me. He has placed her in my life to balance my shortcomings.

Maybe you need the same kind of help in your life of leadership. If you are not generous by nature, ask God to change your heart and add members to your team who are strong where you are weak. Then empower them to be generous on your behalf. Effective leaders strive to be generous with others. They understand the boomerang effect of generosity — it always comes back to you.

ESSENTIAL INSIGHT 11: *Work to develop a generous heart toward others and in doing so, give to yourself.*

12   Bad Taste in Your Mouth

Gossip is a sort of smoke that comes from the dirty tobacco-pipes of those who diffuse it: it proves nothing but the bad taste of the smoker.
— GEORGE ELIOT

PROVERBS 12:13-19

The gossip of bad people gets them in trouble;
>   the conversation of good people keeps them out of it.

Well-spoken words bring satisfaction;
>   well-done work has its own reward.

Fools are headstrong and do what they like;
>   wise people take advice.

Fools have short fuses and explode all too quickly;
>   the prudent quietly shrug off insults.

Truthful witness by a good person clears the air,
>   but liars lay down a smoke screen of deceit.

Rash language cuts and maims,
>   but there is healing in the words of the wise.

Truth lasts;
>   lies are here today, gone tomorrow.

Can you control your tongue? Few have mastered this small part of human anatomy. I have heard it said that the only time some people open their mouth is to change feet! A foot is sure to leave a bad taste in anyone's mouth. The tongue is a powerful force that can be used for good or evil. Try to master yours if you can.

Some leaders don't realize the power of the words coming out of their mouth. Everything they say has an impact just by virtue of their personality and position. And because they are in charge, there is often no one who will point out their faults.

I had a friend in college who was always criticizing others. It got so bad that I found myself thinking about ways to avoid spending any serious time with him. Then it hit me that I had a responsibility to redirect his thinking and behavior. I could be a positive influence in his life that might just help him overcome his negativity. I was truly blessed one day when he commented on the impact I'd had on him. He was greatly impressed by my kind remarks regarding others, so much so that it had caused him to ponder how he could improve upon this in his own life. I had preached a sermon by my behavior and he got the message loud and clear.

When you have something important to say, how do you go about it? When you have something that doesn't need to be said, can you keep your mouth shut? Putting your foot in your mouth is only surpassed in recklessness by cramming your ideas down someone else's throat — both can leave an equally bad taste behind!

ESSENTIAL INSIGHT 12: *Learn to harness the power of your tongue and use it to do the greatest possible good.*

13 Let's Get Real

Whatever is done without ostentation, and without the people being witnesses of it is, in my opinion, most praiseworthy.
— MARCUS TULLIUS CICERO

PROVERBS 13:7-10

A pretentious, showy life is an empty life;
    a plain and simple life is a full life.
The rich can be sued for everything they have,
    but the poor are free of such threats.
The lives of good people are brightly lit streets;
    the lives of the wicked are dark alleys.
Arrogant know-it-alls stir up discord,
    but wise men and women listen to each other's counsel.

Have you ever had an experience where what you saw was NOT what you got? This was my experience when I came face-to-face with the powerhouse wrestler Hulk Hogan.

I met him in Denver when he came to meet Billy Graham at a crusade. The Hulkster was not at all what I expected. Yes, he was tanned, muscular, and huge, but he was also quiet and humble in his demeanor — the polar opposite of the TV persona he had so skillfully crafted over the years.

Underneath all the glamour and facade, humans are all the same — just clay fashioned into housing for a living soul. Everyone is searching for meaning and purpose in life and shares the same basic human needs. Showmanship is one thing, but don't be fooled by your own act. At the heart of it all you are the same as everyone else — no better and no worse. And you need to recognize that fact.

You should neither intimidate others nor be intimidated by the external trappings of success. Attend to the basics — your body, soul, and mind. Cultivate the simple pleasures and have a realistic appraisal of yourself. God doesn't read your press clippings. And if He did, He would not be very impressed.

ESSENTIAL INSIGHT 13: *Drawing attention to yourself may be good for business, but the simple life is good for your soul.*

14   Last to Let You Down

But friendship is precious; not only in the shade, but in the sunshine of life, and thanks to a benevolent arrangement the greater part of life is sunshine.
— THOMAS JEFFERSON

PROVERBS 14:1-8

Lady Wisdom builds a lovely home;
   Sir Fool comes along and tears it down brick by brick.
An honest life shows respect for GOD;
   a degenerate life is a slap in his face.
Frivolous talk provokes a derisive smile;
   wise speech evokes nothing but respect.
No cattle, no crops;
   a good harvest requires a strong ox for the plow.
A true witness never lies;
   a false witness makes a business of it.
Cynics look high and low for wisdom — and never find it;
   the open-minded find it right on their doorstep!
Escape quickly from the company of fools;
   they're a waste of your time, a waste of your words.
The wisdom of the wise keeps life on track;
   the foolishness of fools lands them in the ditch.

When I was a young man just starting out in Christian ministry, an older, wiser man invited me out to lunch because he wanted to have a straight talk with me. He had observed some dangerous tendencies in my life and was willing to point them out to me as a friend. I was crushed. From my vantage point, his observations were wrong, and I was an innocent person. However, in the coming days, weeks, and even years, the truths of his observations were revealed.

That wise man is still my friend today and his words still help me. There were others in my life who I thought were friends, but when I really needed them, they let me down. I even allowed some of them to drag me down with their less than godly character and worldview. Be very careful of the friends you choose. They have a dramatic impact on how you interpret life and everything you do. The same is true of business associates, partners, your spouse, and anyone else you let into your life. If you choose foolish people to share your world with, you will end up a fool as well.

You will need at least six good friends because that's how many it will take to carry your casket to the grave. Quite literally, your friends should be the last to let you down.

ESSENTIAL INSIGHT 14: *Choose your friends carefully.*

15　The Way Up

Humility is the foundation of all the other virtues hence, in the soul in which this virtue does not exist there cannot be any other virtue.

— SAINT AUGUSTINE

PROVERBS 15:10-12,14-17

It's a school of hard knocks for those who leave GOD's path,
　　a dead-end street for those who hate God's rules.
Even hell holds no secrets from GOD —
　　do you think he can't read human hearts?
Know-it-alls don't like being told what to do;
　　they avoid the company of wise men and women.
An intelligent person is always eager to take in more truth;
　　fools feed on fast-food fads and fancies.
A miserable heart means a miserable life;
　　a cheerful heart fills the day with song.
A simple life in the Fear-of-GOD
　　is better than a rich life with a ton of headaches.
Better a bread crust shared in love
　　than a slab of prime rib served in hate.

Sometimes God humbles us to test our reaction before He lifts us up. Have you been embarrassed or ashamed only to discover later that your experience was supremely valuable? Maybe your failure affected your life in such a way that nothing else could have. I don't seem to learn very much when everything is going great. It is usually in my failures that God gets my attention. What about you?

A dear friend of mine was fresh out of college and invited to try out for a professional football team. In college he had been a force to reckon with as a defensive cornerback. But that day my friend was beat time and again by a rookie quarterback and wide-receiver combo who were also hoping to make big-time professional sports. My friend was cut from the team — a little discouraged, yes, but undeterred in his pursuit of excellence. He went on to be a successful Christian layman and attorney with a career that lasted many decades.

I have found that down is the way up. Anyone can handle success. How you handle failure is a sign of greatness. Most leaders will suffer setbacks and discouragement; it goes with the territory if you are trying to accomplish something great. Those who are always playing it safe will never find out what kind of stuff they are made of.

Your failures and disappointments are not always what they appear to be either — they could be just momentary setbacks as you focus in on God's will for your lives. You may have heard of the quarterback who beat my friend that day in tryouts; his name was Bart Starr and the wide-receiver was none other than Raymond Berry — two of the greatest players to ever represent the Green Bay Packers and now both in the NFL Hall of Fame.

ESSENTIAL INSIGHT 15: *Humble yourself before God, and He will lift you up.*

16   If I Knew Then What I Know Now

Let our advance worrying become advance thinking and planning.
— WINSTON CHURCHILL

PROVERBS 16:1-5,9

Mortals make elaborate plans,
    but GOD has the last word.
Humans are satisfied with whatever looks good;
    GOD probes for what *is* good.
Put GOD in charge of your work,
    then what you've planned will take place.
GOD made everything with a place and purpose;
    even the wicked are included — but for *judgment*.
GOD can't stomach arrogance or pretense;
    believe me, he'll put those upstarts in their place.
We plan the way we want to live,
    but only GOD makes us able to live it.

When I was a young man in college, my personal plans were along the lines of playing football for the rest of my life and making a lot of money in the process. Oh, it seems stupid now as I think about it, but that is just the point — I had no plan. I was a kid who still thought in terms of doing what seemed fun at the time and did not think about where my dreams might take me. Well, I grew up, and it took a few hard lessons to do it. How about you?

The most valuable piece of advice I ever received in this regard was from a friend who had worked as a manager in the business world and gone into Christian ministry later in life. He told me that even the biggest tasks can be broken down into small pieces that are manageable. Your life's goals can be broken into bite-sized chunks that are not so difficult to achieve.

First, you need to decide what you want to accomplish and work back from there to where you are now. My first goal in life has always been to serve God in some way. I think you will agree — that is a big task. When I finally got serious about making a plan for my life, I decided to seek out someone who was doing what I wanted to do and learn from them. So I did just that and one thing led to another, and here I am. Did you notice that I focused on "what" I wanted to do, not "how" I would do it? "How" is in God's hands.

ESSENTIAL INSIGHT 16: *When you make your plans, don't leave God out of the formula. That is the only part that makes any sense.*

17   The King of Virtues

Forgiveness is the answer to the child's dream of a miracle by which what is broken is made whole again, what is soiled is made clean again.

— DAG HAMMARSKJÖLD

PROVERBS 17:1,9,14,17

A meal of bread and water in contented peace
   is better than a banquet spiced with quarrels.
Overlook an offense and bond a friendship;
   fasten on to a slight and — good-bye, friend!
The start of a quarrel is like a leak in a dam,
   so stop it before it bursts.
Friends love through all kinds of weather,
   and families stick together in all kinds of trouble.

I n my opinion, Coretta Scott King was the epitome of forgiveness. When I was living in Atlanta, I had the opportunity to meet her and tour her late husband's museum. If anyone had the right to be bitter and resentful in this life, it was Coretta Scott King; however, she impressed me with her resolve to take all the negativity and turn it into a positive force for the sake of the oppressed and downtrodden.

I have witnessed a lot of misery suffered by people who have been abused and hurt by the powers of this world. When we feel we have been cheated by life, we make a choice to allow ourselves to become bitter and withdrawn or we can decide to learn from the experience and become better.

When I was sixteen, my parents divorced and my world appeared to come apart at the seams. It made me angry to think that I had been cheated out of my right to be happy. But this was not the end of my life as I supposed. It was merely a temporary detour that eventually helped me move in a more positive direction. Psychologists tell us that it is the way we choose to interpret what happens in our lives, more than the actual circumstances and experiences, that determines our destiny. Bitter or better — we get to decide!

Here is my observation: It is the one who has been wronged who has all the power, not the one who does the wrong. And our power comes in the form of forgiveness. When we forgive, we liberate ourselves to live the life God has given us.

ESSENTIAL INSIGHT 17: *Forgiveness is a powerful force in the hands of those who have been wronged.*

18 Great Escape

I like to listen. I have learned a great deal from listening carefully. Most people never listen.

— ERNEST HEMINGWAY

PROVERBS 18:13-17

Answering before listening
 is both stupid and rude.
A healthy spirit conquers adversity,
 but what can you do when the spirit is crushed?
Wise men and women are always learning,
 always listening for fresh insights.
A gift gets attention;
 it buys the attention of eminent people.
The first speech in a court case is always convincing —
 until the cross-examination starts!

L eaders know that being a good listener can lead to the opportunity to say something that may powerfully affect another life.

One memory that continually blesses me is that of Steve McQueen sitting in the balcony of a California church drinking up every word of the gospel as he carefully followed along in his Bible.

Steve had a love for vintage aircraft. His gifted flight instructor was a quiet Christian man of few words. Over the weeks Steve and his instructor spent a lot of time together in the cockpit of his plane. During that time Steve noticed there was something unusual about his instructor, so he asked him what it was. Up to now the old saint had mostly listened to Steve and only dropped in an occasional word of wisdom. He took Steve to see his pastor, who told him what it meant to know Christ personally. That day Steve McQueen invited Jesus into his heart.

At one point in his life Steve had all the answers and was not asking anyone for guidance. But because of a Christian who was a good listener, his heart changed and he became like a sponge ready to soak up any advice that might bring more meaning to his life.

Steve McQueen's final days were spent battling cancer. At the end, he was found dead in his bed with a Bible opened on his chest. Steve had become a good listener to the life-giving words of God.

ESSENTIAL INSIGHT 18: *Learn to listen and discover life.*

19 Never Give Up!

Paralyze resistance with persistence.
— WOODY HAYES

PROVERBS 19:7

When you're down on your luck, even your family avoids you —
   yes, even your best friends wish you'd get lost.
If they see you coming, they look the other way —
   out of sight, out of mind.

The leadership of Winston Churchill, Abraham Lincoln, and Teddy Roosevelt always inspires me because they knew how to overcome great obstacles through steady persistence. These men are my heroes. I like them because they inspire me to be persistent in the face of adversity. They never gave up!

When I was in college, I almost gave up. Two summers in a row I almost didn't return to college to finish my degree. Money was tight and I was lacking direction. Why should I try so hard when I didn't even know what I was going to do with my education?

But God spoke to my heart each time, and I became convinced that if I prepared, He would give me the opportunity I needed. I thought my success might come in sports but it didn't. And as I lay in my hospital bed after two consecutive surgeries on my knee, I finally gave up on that dream and began to despair. Has that ever happened to you?

But slowly God began to build me back up after my lost hope. He reminded me that my life was never really about sports — they had just been an avenue to build my character — He had bigger plans for me. So with His help I started over and regained my confidence to move ahead by faith.

By the end of my senior year, I had a degree and a job, and I have never looked back. Sports were not my long-term place of service, but they were an important schoolroom for me. The lessons I learned have served me well. God may change your direction but He will not abandon you. If you persist, you will discover the purpose He has designed for your life and that will bring you more satisfaction than you can possibly imagine. Never give up!

ESSENTIAL INSIGHT 19: *Never give up, no matter how dark the clouds over your head. God has a plan for you that will bring unsurpassed joy to your life.*

20 Anger Management 101

Anger makes dull men witty, but it keeps them poor.
— FRANCIS BACON

PROVERBS 20:1-3

Wine makes you mean, beer makes you quarrelsome —
    a staggering drunk is not much fun.
Quick-tempered leaders are like mad dogs —
    cross them and they bite your head off.
It's a mark of good character to avert quarrels,
    but fools love to pick fights.

As a leader, I know that clear and effective communication is important. What does anger communicate to you? To me it communicates a lack of self-control and frustration.

As a young athlete, most of my coaches used the "angry screamer" approach to coaching. This is essentially a lot of yelling and intimidation but very little, if any, actual coaching. A coach is supposed to tell you how to do something, show you how to do it, and then encourage you to do it yourself repeatedly until you get it right.

Think about how God works as your coach. He gives us the information through His Word, shows us how to do it by the many examples in history and through leaders, and then He lets us go out and try it. Consequently, there is a lot of failure among followers of Christ. I expect believers around me to fail — don't you? That tells me they are learning and trying new things.

So when we fail, God is not angry. He just helps us get back on our feet and lets us try again — sometimes without learning our lesson because that is up to us. He can only create the opportunity for us to learn — He does not control how we will process it.

When any leader lets anger get out of control, he can lose credibility. So if you are angry, watch out! It can have some serious consequences and can actually cause your team to fail. I never met a successful leader who could not control his temper. Uncontrolled anger is a sign of weakness — not leadership.

ESSENTIAL INSIGHT 20: *Your uncontrolled anger may give you a moment of satisfaction but a lifetime of regret.*

21   Living Fully Alive

Productivity is never an accident. It is always the result of a commitment to excellence, intelligent planning and focused effort.
— PAUL MEYER

PROVERBS 21:1-5

Good leadership is a channel of water controlled by GOD;
>   he directs it to whatever ends he chooses.

We justify our actions by appearances;
>   GOD examines our motives.

Clean living before GOD and justice with our neighbors
>   mean far more to GOD than religious performance.

Arrogance and pride — distinguishing marks in the wicked —
>   are just plain sin.

Careful planning puts you ahead in the long run;
>   hurry and scurry puts you further behind.

A wise man once pointed out to me that the most active animal in the barnyard is a chicken that has just had its head cut off. Merely generating a lot of activity is not necessarily a sign of life. From time to time I have been confused on this point, and I let others dictate to me how I should conduct myself. They made me believe that if I was not very busy, I was not capable of being productive. What is true success? How do we get it? How do we maintain it?

Let's start by coming up with a new model for success that does not necessarily equate activity with productivity. While it is true that you will never accomplish anything without doing something, it is also true that too much busyness can actually blur our ability to think strategically and use your resources to their greatest advantage.

Learn how to say "NO." Be thoughtful about the tasks you undertake and use your skills and gifts effectively to accomplish what only you may be able to do while letting others do what they can do. Leadership sometimes means slowing down and being strategic in activity.

I have often had responsibility for running large events. The first thing I try to do is assess my resources and determine how to leverage them to the greatest advantage. Time is often your most limited resource. Look at the time available to accomplish the task. Decide how to best use your effort in the available time and work backward from the deadlines to the present situation. Stop and think so you can think of stopping.

If you want to build something that has a real life of its own, focus on your true objective and breathe life into your effort through strategic planning.

ESSENTIAL INSIGHT 21: *Mere activity is not necessarily a sign of life.*

22   Stop. Look. Listen.

Genius always gives its best at first; prudence, at last.
— LUCIUS ANNAEUS SENECA

PROVERBS 22:26-27

Don't gamble on the pot of gold at the end of the rainbow,
   hocking your house against a lucky chance.
The time will come when you have to pay up;
   you'll be left with nothing but the shirt on your back.

D o you have a tendency to leap into situations without weighing them carefully? That can be a good thing if a person is lying on the side of the road, bleeding to death, and in need of immediate assistance. However, being impulsive can be fatal if in your haste you are run over by oncoming traffic. Control your impulses and respond prudently.

The writer of Proverbs warns against being imprudent. A careful person will not be right in every decision he or she makes, but will not enter into any decision too lightly either. The prudent person understands that everything does not turn out the way it seems it will at first glance. So think your decisions through, especially the ones with wider implications.

President Jimmy Carter was proud to be known as a peanut farmer from Plains, Georgia. I first met him in 1994 and was impressed with how fit and alert he was for a man of his years. He was one of the most diligent and hardworking leaders we have ever had in the White House, but he has not always been known for his prudence. I well remember the high-stakes gamble he wagered in calling together the leaders of Egypt and Israel that resulted in the astounding success of the Camp David Accords.

But President Carter was also responsible for the daring, but failed, rescue attempt of the Iranian hostages in 1980, which resulted in a fiasco for the would-be rescuers. President Carter was not afraid to take chances but they didn't always result in success. The wise caution of Proverbs to exercise prudence is not mere peanuts — it could change the way people think about you — so be prudent.

ESSENTIAL INSIGHT 22: *Weigh your decisions carefully. You can smear a lifetime of accomplishment with doubt in a moment of haste.*

23 A Royal Pain

Appearances to the mind are of four kinds. Things either are what they appear to be; or they neither are, nor appear to be; or they are, and do not appear to be; or they are not, and yet appear to be. Rightly to aim in all these cases is the wise man's task.

— EPICTETUS

PROVERBS 23:1-8

When you go out to dinner with an influential person,
    mind your manners:
Don't gobble your food,
    don't talk with your mouth full.
And don't stuff yourself;
    bridle your appetite.
Don't wear yourself out trying to get rich;
    restrain yourself!
Riches disappear in the blink of an eye;
    wealth sprouts wings
    and flies off into the wild blue yonder.
Don't accept a meal from a tightwad;
    don't expect anything special.
He'll be as stingy with you as he is with himself;
    he'll say, "Eat! Drink!" but won't mean a word of it.
His miserly serving will turn your stomach
    when you realize the meal's a sham.

E ven Epictetus seems confused about appearances. Don't build your life around trying to impress those who have power and wealth or hoping to become one of the elite of our society. Underneath the surface, we are all equal before God. Appearances are not only confusing, they can be misleading too.

My wife and I had the opportunity to worship with the Queen of England and her youngest sons in her private chapel in Great Windsor Park just outside of London. She sat in a private curtained box made especially for such occasions. At the end of the service she carefully positioned herself in front of the main exit and greeted guests as they left, just as a pastor might do at the end of the service. When our turn came, we did not shake hands with the Queen because it is not considered proper to touch a royal personage without being invited to do so. It must be painful to be so concerned about appearances and formalities.

The One whose appearances are real has chosen to be humble and meek — His name is Jesus. Yes, every knee will bow and every tongue confess that He is Lord. But He called us friends and laid aside the prerogatives of royalty when He tore down the curtain of separation in the Temple and gave us direct access to His Father by faith through His death and resurrection.

Weak men may insist on status, formality, and appearances, but God sees us for what we are. Wise leaders follow the example of Christ's humility. They are aware that under the surface they are just like everyone else — no better and no worse.

ESSENTIAL INSIGHT 23: *Look beneath the surface — people and circumstances are not always what they appear to be.*

24 Marley's Chains

He was born in a humble cottage nine miles from Alexandrea in the parish of St.
Ann. He lived in the western section of Kingston as a boy where he joined in the
struggle of the ghetto. He learned the message of survival in his boyhood days in
Kingston's west end. But it was his raw talent, unswerving discipline and sheer
perseverance that transported him from just another victim of the ghetto to the
top ranking superstar in the entertainment industry of the third world.

— EDWARD SEAGA, JAMAICAN PRESIDENT, MAY 1981 AT
   BOB MARLEY'S FUNERAL

PROVERBS 24:1-6,19-20

Don't envy bad people;
> don't even want to be around them.

All they think about is causing a disturbance;
> all they talk about is making trouble.

It takes wisdom to build a house,
> and understanding to set it on a firm foundation;

It takes knowledge to furnish its rooms
> with fine furniture and beautiful draperies.

It's better to be wise than strong;
> intelligence outranks muscle any day.

Strategic planning is the key to warfare;
> to win, you need a lot of good counsel.

Don't bother your head with braggarts
> or wish you could succeed like the wicked.

Those people have no future at all;
> they're headed down a dead-end street.

B ob Marley, the Jamaican-born reggae singer who died of cancer in 1981, was one of the most interesting men I almost met. I was working in Jamaica and felt inspired to go see this modern urban rebel at his white mansion in Kingston surrounded by high walls. At the front gate I encountered one of his associates who told me Marley was on tour. So I left him a personal note and a copy of Billy Graham's book *Peace with God*. Later I discovered he was actually receiving medical care for the fatal disease that took his life a few months later.

I don't know if Bob Marley ever received my gift or if he read about how to have peace with God, but I do know that he was loved by the God who pursued him to the very end. Christ can set you free of the chains that hold you in captivity and keep you from living your life as He intended. Your faith in Christ is the key to the lock that holds your chains in place.

Bob Marley's talent and fame caused many to applaud and even envy him. But too soon he had to face death just like you and I will someday. I am confident his chains of death would now be gladly exchanged for longer life and inner peace. Fame and talent are nothing compared to the value of our precious soul. Our chains of worldly success may seem like good things at the time, but they will bind us to death if we let them.

ESSENTIAL INSIGHT 24: *Don't envy the success of the world — it is like a chain of death.*

25 A Home Run

Our ambition should be to rule ourselves, the true kingdom for each one of us;
and true progress is to know more, and be more, and to do more.
— OSCAR WILDE

PROVERBS 25:4-7

Remove impurities from the silver
   and the silversmith can craft a fine chalice;
Remove the wicked from leadership
   and authority will be credible and God-honoring.
Don't work yourself into the spotlight;
   don't push your way into the place of prominence.
It's better to be promoted to a place of honor
   than face humiliation by being demoted.

What is your greatest ambition? A close friend of mine has suffered all his life from the frustration of unrealized dreams. Oh, there is nothing wrong with healthy discontent but we cannot always live in the world of our aspirations; sometimes we must live in the world of our present circumstances. Has your ambition gotten you down? Are you angry with God for the realities you face from day to day? Do you need a way out of your failure and disappointment?

Merlyn Mantle once allowed me to visit her home and showed me the personal trophy case of her husband, all-time baseball great, Mickey Mantle. As a young boy I was mesmerized by his contest with Roger Maris to break the home-run record set by Babe Ruth.

I was breathless as I took in the amazing souvenirs of this baseball icon. I asked Mrs. Mantle which of all her husband's trophies was his most prized. I thought it would be one of his many batting trophies; but to my surprise it was the MVP award given by his New York Yankee teammates. This was because it was given by those whom he most wished to serve — the members of his own team. For "the Mic" it was not what he thought of himself or what strangers thought of him but what his own teammates believed about him that mattered most. Now that's a sure way to hit home runs!

ESSENTIAL INSIGHT 25: *Always do your best, knowing that God will lift you up and never let you fail.*

26 A Slice of Heaven

In time of peace prepare for war.
— FLAVIUS RENATUS VEGETIUS

PROVERBS 26:17-21

You grab a mad dog by the ears
    when you butt into a quarrel that's none of your business.
People who shrug off deliberate deceptions,
    saying, "I didn't mean it, I was only joking,"
Are worse than careless campers
    who walk away from smoldering campfires.
When you run out of wood, the fire goes out;
    when the gossip ends, the quarrel dies down.
A quarrelsome person in a dispute
    is like kerosene thrown on a fire.

Andrew Carnegie founded the Peace Palace and its library at The Hague in the Netherlands with a gift of one and a half million dollars in 1903 — all in an effort to inspire world peace. If you go to their website today and search for "Bible" you will get fifteen hits, and none of them is a real "Bible." Can you imagine that? They have a library devoted to peace and not a single Bible, the greatest book ever written on the subject of peace.

Peace will always be an elusive dream unless we first meet the Prince of Peace, Jesus Christ Himself. It is Christ who can give us the serenity to be kind in the face of adversity; it is Christ who gives us the ability to remain silent in response to angry words spewed in our face; and it is Christ alone who will someday bring peace to humanity when He establishes His kingdom on earth as it is in heaven.

Submit to the peace of Christ. Let Him calm your inner person. You can be a calming influence on others if you are filled with inner peace. Peace flows from the heart. Tune in to the peace of heaven. As Christ said to the Samaritan woman at the well, "Anyone who drinks the water I give will never thirst — not ever. The water I give will be an artesian spring within, gushing fountains of endless life" (John 4:13).

ESSENTIAL INSIGHT 26: *As much as is within you, be at peace with all men.*

27 Love Hurts

Why love if losing hurts so much? I have no answers anymore; only the life I have lived. The pain now is part of the happiness then.
— ANTHONY HOPKINS IN *SHADOWLANDS*

PROVERBS 27:5-9

A spoken reprimand is better
>   than approval that's never expressed.
The wounds from a lover are worth it;
>   kisses from an enemy do you in.
When you've stuffed yourself, you refuse dessert;
>   when you're starved, you could eat a horse.
People who won't settle down, wandering hither and yon,
>   are like restless birds, flitting to and fro.
Just as lotions and fragrance give sensual delight,
>   a sweet friendship refreshes the soul.

Any young lover who has failed in love will immediately agree that love can hurt. But after the wound has healed a little, they will also be the first to try to love again because of the joy it brings.

I remember my first love. It was immature, painful, wonderful, and hopeless all at the same time. When it failed, I could have just given up on love or learned from it and looked harder for a better, more satisfying relationship next time.

I chose the latter and I'm so glad I did. Several years later I found the love of my life, and we now have been married for twenty-five years. It has not always been easy. In fact there have been moments when I am sure my wife has wondered how she could be so unhappy. But those thoughts were only momentary and the shared joys have been immense and overflowing.

I'm no saint to live with. And my sweet wife has consistently blessed me by loving me through thick and thin. Her honest advice may hurt some times, but I can always depend on it. She has given me everything she has to give, and together we have two amazing children as the culmination of our union of love and commitment.

Love hurts — but it is well worth the pain and sacrifice. Nothing has given me more to live for than the love I have found with my wife and family. These are the ones closest to me, and no matter what happens, I can trust them with my life. Look for love, live for love, and you will find it. But in order to keep love, you must give it away.

ESSENTIAL INSIGHT 27: *Give yourself to those you love; trust them to be faithful and accept their input into your life as you would any other act of love.*

28 Little Is Much When God Is in It

Don't judge each day by the harvest you reap, but by the seeds you plant.
— ROBERT STEVENSON

PROVERBS 28:18-20

Walk straight — live well and be saved;
    a devious life is a doomed life.
Work your garden — you'll end up with plenty of food;
    play and party — you'll end up with an empty plate.
Committed and persistent work pays off;
    get-rich-quick schemes are ripoffs.

Success does not happen overnight. It is the result of faithfulness in little things over a lifetime. The small unnoticed things can add up to great achievement and a crescendo of success — if you are persistent. You can build your life on a consistent body of small achievements, not just a single giant success.

I met Jim Ryun in 1980 in California. As the world record holder in the mile run for many years, he knew what it meant to reap the benefits of multitudes of hours invested over a long period of time. You do not become a world-class runner without a lot of practice and self-discipline. As I listened to his story, I was amazed because his personal life paralleled his running career. It is rare for anything of great worth to come easily, even to the very gifted.

The day came when Jim's record was finally broken by an eighteen-year-old from Virginia. What if all Jim Ryun had to be proud of was a thirty-six-year-old running record that now had been broken by a high school senior? He would never recover; his running career would be over as well as his feeling of accomplishment. But Jim Ryun has something more — a body of service to the Lord and his community that has spanned a lifetime. Yes, his fame gave him a platform, but it could have been a very dangerous place to stand if it was all he had ever accomplished. Now he is on much firmer and safer ground surrounded by a lifetime of achievement. You reap what you sow. Sow generously and you will reap generously. Sow sparingly and you will find yourself impoverished when you meet the grim reaper.

ESSENTIAL INSIGHT 28: *Don't put all your eggs in one basket. Sow many acts of value over your lifetime, and you will be amazed at the harvest when you are old.*

29 Can't Get There from Here

The value of marriage is not that adults produce children but that children produce adults.

— PETER DE VRIES

PROVERBS 29:15,17,21,26

Wise discipline imparts wisdom;
    spoiled adolescents embarrass their parents.
Discipline your children; you'll be glad you did —
    they'll turn out delightful to live with.
If you let people treat you like a doormat,
    you'll be quite forgotten in the end.
Everyone tries to get help from the leader,
    but only GOD will give us justice.

Sometimes there are tricks of the trade that others are willing to pass on to save a little time and energy along the way. But when it comes to leading others, there aren't any shortcuts. Take the example of raising your children. Discipline is a vital ingredient in the recipe of parenting. We all need to learn to bend to authority. That was man's basic failure in the Garden of Eden, and we continue to make the same mistake today.

Cross-grain investors on Wall Street have made a fortune out of seeing which way the masses are moving and doing just the opposite. A leader often has the same opportunity by cutting across the grain of conventional wisdom. The masses say that discipline of our children will break their spirit, but the wise leader knows this is not the case. Discipline will make your child into the adult you want them to be.

It is not easy to say "no" to those under our authority, especially if we care about them. But their short-term gratification is not worth the long-term disappointment of a ruined life and a hardened heart.

Some of the worst failures I have seen in parenting have been committed by successful leaders who would never treat their employees so carelessly. Only God can help you do what is right and pass on a blessing to your children that will last a lifetime. Trying to take any shortcuts in this process of training will only prove to be frustrating. Dead ends often look like shortcuts, but you can't get where you want to be by taking them.

ESSENTIAL INSIGHT 29: *An effective leader knows how to manage those under his authority and has the will to do what is right for them.*

30   Two Blind Men

Money is the barometer of a society's virtue.
— AYN RAND

PROVERBS 30:8-9

Give me enough food to live on,
     neither too much nor too little.
If I'm too full, I might get independent,
     saying, "God? Who needs him?"
If I'm poor, I might steal
     and dishonor the name of my God.

What do all men have in common? One thing is the love of money and dependence on it. This vice affects the rich as well as the poor. The rich are burdened by how to keep wealth and the poor are haunted by how to get wealth. To both groups, money can be a curse that plagues them all their lives and affects the way they see things.

How do we balance our spiritual lives with the needs of the material world? A rich man can be poor spiritually and a poor man can be rich in his inner being. What drives you? I know very few wealthy men who are truly "rich" and yet I know many poor folk who truly are independently wealthy in their soul.

I sat behind Ray Charles on a flight to California one day and was amazed to see how he traveled all alone and managed quite well, not just for a sightless person, but for any person at all. Sitting next to me was a very intelligent businessman who was not managing so well. He appeared to have it all materially, but seemed to be missing the spiritual insight to recognize his personal need of a Savior. Two blind men; one physically blind and the other spiritually sightless. Which would you rather be?

We live in a world of contrasts. I have noticed that money can cause a sort of blindness that is difficult to overcome for any man. It makes us self-reliant and creates an illusion of being self-sustaining. A wise leader knows that adequate funding does not make us successful any more than having eyes enables us to see. Blindness has many forms. How is your sight?

ESSENTIAL INSIGHT 30: *Don't let your love of money blind you to what is truly important or valuable. Money is only a tool — it doesn't make you rich.*

31 A Perfect Picture of Leadership

Excellence is doing ordinary things extraordinarily well.
— JOHN W. GARDNER

PROVERBS 31:10-12,28-29

A good woman is hard to find,
    and worth far more than diamonds.
Her husband trusts her without reserve,
    and never has reason to regret it.
Never spiteful, she treats him generously
    all her life long.
Her children respect and bless her;
    her husband joins in with words of praise:
"Many women have done wonderful things,
    but you've outclassed them all!"

L eaders know excellence when they see it. And the writer of these verses saw it in the life of the woman described here. What is the value of excellence? Excellence inspires trust, loyalty, and respect and establishes a reputation that will follow you wherever you go and as long as you live. The woman in these verses led in a family context and did it with excellence. What "family" are you being called to lead? God desires excellence from you, no matter what your situation.

I was raised in a suburb, part of a conservative Christian family and the son of a medical doctor. I was very large as a child and found it difficult to fit in. I scored low on social graces and felt the pain of my situation constantly.

At times I was full of sorrow and angry with God for the burdens He had placed on me. Then I realized that this is who I was and where I was. Could the uniqueness of my life be seen as a gift and actually be vital for the adult and leader God intended me to become? I asked God to begin to show me how to live out my life in my situation, and this was a major turning point for me.

The woman of Proverbs 31 excelled in whatever she was given to do each day. God gives her to us by way of Scripture to show us excellence, strength, and beauty. It is a perfect picture of what God wants from His leaders in all walks of life; be the person He created you to be and excel regardless of your situation.

ESSENTIAL INSIGHT 31: *Celebrate excellence and discover God's world of opportunity.*

PROVERBS

WISE SAYINGS OF SOLOMON

A MANUAL FOR LIVING

1-6 These are the wise sayings of Solomon,
David's son, Israel's king —
Written down so we'll know how to live well and right,
to understand what life means and where it's going;
A manual for living,
for learning what's right and just and fair;
To teach the inexperienced the ropes
and give our young people a grasp on reality.
There's something here also for seasoned men and women,
still a thing or two for the experienced to learn —
Fresh wisdom to probe and penetrate,
the rhymes and reasons of wise men and women.

START WITH GOD

7 Start with GOD — the first step in learning is bowing down to GOD;
only fools thumb their noses at such wisdom and learning.

8-19 Pay close attention, friend, to what your father tells you;
never forget what you learned at your mother's knee.
Wear their counsel like flowers in your hair,
like rings on your fingers.
Dear friend, if bad companions tempt you,
don't go along with them.
If they say — "Let's go out and raise some hell.
Let's beat up some old man, mug some old woman.
Let's pick them clean
and get them ready for their funerals.
We'll load up on top-quality loot.
We'll haul it home by the truckload.
Join us for the time of your life!
With us, it's share and share alike!" —
Oh, friend, don't give them a second look;
don't listen to them for a minute.
They're racing to a very bad end,
hurrying to ruin everything they lay hands on.
Nobody robs a bank
with everyone watching,

Yet that's what these people are doing —
    they're doing themselves in.
When you grab all you can get, that's what happens:
    the more you get, the less you are.

LADY WISDOM

20-21   Lady Wisdom goes out in the street and shouts.
    At the town center she makes her speech.
In the middle of the traffic she takes her stand.
    At the busiest corner she calls out:

22-24   "Simpletons! How long will you wallow in ignorance?
    Cynics! How long will you feed your cynicism?
Idiots! How long will you refuse to learn?
    About face! I can revise your life.
Look, I'm ready to pour out my spirit on you;
    I'm ready to tell you all I know.
As it is, I've called, but you've turned a deaf ear;
    I've reached out to you, but you've ignored me.

25-28   "Since you laugh at my counsel
    and make a joke of my advice,
How can I take you seriously?
    I'll turn the tables and joke about *your* troubles!
What if the roof falls in,
    and your whole life goes to pieces?
What if catastrophe strikes and there's nothing
    to show for your life but rubble and ashes?
You'll need me then. You'll call for me, but don't expect
        an answer.
    No matter how hard you look, you won't find me.

29-33   "Because you hated Knowledge
    and had nothing to do with the Fear-of-GOD,
Because you wouldn't take my advice
    and brushed aside all my offers to train you,
Well, you've made your bed — now lie in it;
    you wanted your own way — now, how do you like it?
Don't you see what happens, you simpletons, you idiots?
    Carelessness kills; complacency is murder.
First pay attention to me, and then relax.
    Now you can take it easy — you're in good hands."

MAKE INSIGHT YOUR PRIORITY

1-5   Good friend, take to heart what I'm telling you;
    collect my counsels and guard them with your life.
Tune your ears to the world of Wisdom;
    set your heart on a life of Understanding.
That's right — if you make Insight your priority,
    and won't take no for an answer,
Searching for it like a prospector panning for gold,
    like an adventurer on a treasure hunt,
Believe me, before you know it Fear-of-GOD will be yours;
    you'll have come upon the Knowledge of God.

6-8   And here's why: GOD gives out Wisdom free,
    is plainspoken in Knowledge and Understanding.
He's a rich mine of Common Sense for those who live well,
    a personal bodyguard to the candid and sincere.
He keeps his eye on all who live honestly,
    and pays special attention to his loyally committed ones.

9-15   So now you can pick out what's true and fair,
    find all the good trails!
Lady Wisdom will be your close friend,
    and Brother Knowledge your pleasant companion.
Good Sense will scout ahead for danger,
    Insight will keep an eye out for you.
They'll keep you from making wrong turns,
    or following the bad directions
Of those who are lost themselves
    and can't tell a trail from a tumbleweed,
These losers who make a game of evil
    and throw parties to celebrate perversity,
Traveling paths that go nowhere,
    wandering in a maze of detours and dead ends.

16-19   Wise friends will rescue you from the Temptress —
    that smooth-talking Seductress
Who's faithless to the husband she married years ago,
    never gave a second thought to her promises before God.
Her whole way of life is doomed;
    every step she takes brings her closer to hell.
No one who joins her company ever comes back,
    ever sets foot on the path to real living.

20-22 So — join the company of good men and women,
    keep your feet on the tried-and-true paths.
It's the men who walk straight who will settle this land,
    the women with integrity who will last here.
The corrupt will lose their lives;
    the dishonest will be gone for good.

DON'T ASSUME YOU KNOW IT ALL

1-2 **3** Good friend, don't forget all I've taught you;
    take to heart my commands.
They'll help you live a long, long time,
a long life lived full and well.

3-4 Don't lose your grip on Love and Loyalty.
    Tie them around your neck; carve their initials on your heart.
Earn a reputation for living well
    in God's eyes and the eyes of the people.

5-12 Trust GOD from the bottom of your heart;
    don't try to figure out everything on your own.
Listen for GOD's voice in everything you do, everywhere you go;
    he's the one who will keep you on track.
Don't assume that you know it all.
    Run to GOD! Run from evil!
Your body will glow with health,
    your very bones will vibrate with life!
Honor GOD with everything you own;
    give him the first and the best.
Your barns will burst,
    your wine vats will brim over.
But don't, dear friend, resent GOD's discipline;
    don't sulk under his loving correction.
It's the child he loves that GOD corrects;
    a father's delight is behind all this.

THE VERY TREE OF LIFE

13-18 You're blessed when you meet Lady Wisdom,
    when you make friends with Madame Insight.
She's worth far more than money in the bank;
    her friendship is better than a big salary.
Her value exceeds all the trappings of wealth;
    nothing you could wish for holds a candle to her.

With one hand she gives long life,
  with the other she confers recognition.
Her manner is beautiful,
  her life wonderfully complete.
She's the very Tree of Life to those who embrace her.
  Hold her tight — and be blessed!

19-20   With Lady Wisdom, GOD formed Earth;
  with Madame Insight, he raised Heaven.
They knew when to signal rivers and springs to the surface,
  and dew to descend from the night skies.

NEVER WALK AWAY

21-26   Dear friend, guard Clear Thinking and Common Sense with your life;
  don't for a minute lose sight of them.
They'll keep your soul alive and well,
  they'll keep you fit and attractive.
You'll travel safely,
  you'll neither tire nor trip.
You'll take afternoon naps without a worry,
  you'll enjoy a good night's sleep.
No need to panic over alarms or surprises,
  or predictions that doomsday's just around the corner,
Because GOD will be right there with you;
  he'll keep you safe and sound.

27-29   Never walk away from someone who deserves help;
  your hand is *God's* hand for that person.
Don't tell your neighbor "Maybe some other time"
  or "Try me tomorrow"
  when the money's right there in your pocket.
Don't figure ways of taking advantage of your neighbor
  when he's sitting there trusting and unsuspecting.

30-32   Don't walk around with a chip on your shoulder,
  always spoiling for a fight.
Don't try to be like those who shoulder their way through life.
  Why be a bully?
"Why not?" you say. Because GOD can't stand twisted souls.
  It's the straightforward who get his respect.

33-35   GOD's curse blights the house of the wicked,
  but he blesses the home of the righteous.

He gives proud skeptics a cold shoulder,
  but if you're down on your luck, he's right there to help.
Wise living gets rewarded with honor;
  stupid living gets the booby prize.

YOUR LIFE IS AT STAKE

1-2 **4** Listen, friends, to some fatherly advice;
  sit up and take notice so you'll know how to live.
I'm giving you good counsel;
don't let it go in one ear and out the other.

3-9 When I was a boy at my father's knee,
  the pride and joy of my mother,
He would sit me down and drill me:
  "Take this to heart. Do what I tell you — live!
Sell everything and buy Wisdom! Forage for Understanding!
  Don't forget one word! Don't deviate an inch!
Never walk away from Wisdom — she guards your life;
  love her — she keeps her eye on you.
Above all and before all, do this: Get Wisdom!
  Write this at the top of your list: Get Understanding!
Throw your arms around her — believe me, you won't regret it;
  never let her go — she'll make your life glorious.
She'll garland your life with grace,
  she'll festoon your days with beauty."

10-15 Dear friend, take my advice;
  it will add years to your life.
I'm writing out clear directions to Wisdom Way,
  I'm drawing a map to Righteous Road.
I don't want you ending up in blind alleys,
  or wasting time making wrong turns.
Hold tight to good advice; don't relax your grip.
  Guard it well — your life is at stake!
Don't take Wicked Bypass;
  don't so much as set foot on that road.
Stay clear of it; give it a wide berth.
  Make a detour and be on your way.

16-17 Evil people are restless
  unless they're making trouble;

They can't get a good night's sleep
    unless they've made life miserable for somebody.
Perversity is their food and drink,
    violence their drug of choice.

18-19   The ways of right-living people glow with light;
    the longer they live, the brighter they shine.
But the road of wrongdoing gets darker and darker —
    travelers can't see a thing; they fall flat on their faces.

LEARN IT BY HEART

20-22   Dear friend, listen well to my words;
    tune your ears to my voice.
Keep my message in plain view at all times.
    Concentrate! Learn it by heart!
Those who discover these words live, really live;
    body and soul, they're bursting with health.

23-27   Keep vigilant watch over your heart;
    that's where life starts.
Don't talk out of both sides of your mouth;
    avoid careless banter, white lies, and gossip.
Keep your eyes straight ahead;
    ignore all sideshow distractions.
Watch your step,
    and the road will stretch out smooth before you.
Look neither right nor left;
    leave evil in the dust.

NOTHING BUT SIN AND BONES

1-2   **5** Dear friend, pay close attention to this, my wisdom;
    listen very closely to the way I see it.
Then you'll acquire a taste for good sense;
    what I tell you will keep you out of trouble.

3-6   The lips of a seductive woman are oh so sweet,
    her soft words are oh so smooth.
But it won't be long before she's gravel in your mouth,
    a pain in your gut, a wound in your heart.
She's dancing down the primrose path to Death;
    she's headed straight for Hell and taking you with her.

She hasn't a clue about Real Life,
about who she is or where she's going.

7-14   So, my friend, listen closely;
don't treat my words casually.
Keep your distance from such a woman;
absolutely stay out of her neighborhood.
You don't want to squander your wonderful life,
to waste your precious life among the hardhearted.
Why should you allow strangers to take advantage of you?
Why be exploited by those who care nothing for you?
You don't want to end your life full of regrets,
nothing but sin and bones,
Saying, "Oh, why didn't I do what they told me?
Why did I reject a disciplined life?
Why didn't I listen to my mentors,
or take my teachers seriously?
My life is ruined!
I haven't one blessed thing to show for my life!"

NEVER TAKE LOVE FOR GRANTED

15-16   Do you know the saying, "Drink from your own rain barrel,
draw water from your own spring-fed well"?
It's true. Otherwise, you may one day come home
and find your barrel empty and your well polluted.

17-20   Your spring water is for you and you only,
not to be passed around among strangers.
Bless your fresh-flowing fountain!
Enjoy the wife you married as a young man!
Lovely as an angel, beautiful as a rose —
don't ever quit taking delight in her body.
Never take her love for granted!
Why would you trade enduring intimacies for cheap thrills with a whore?
for dalliance with a promiscuous stranger?

21-23   Mark well that GOD doesn't miss a move you make;
he's aware of every step you take.
The shadow of your sin will overtake you;
you'll find yourself stumbling all over yourself in the dark.

Death is the reward of an undisciplined life;
　　your foolish decisions trap you in a dead end.

LIKE A DEER FROM THE HUNTER

1-5　6 Dear friend, if you've gone into hock with your neighbor
　　or locked yourself into a deal with a stranger,
　　If you've impulsively promised the shirt off your back
　　and now find yourself shivering out in the cold,
Friend, don't waste a minute, get yourself out of that mess.
　　You're in that man's clutches!
　　Go, put on a long face; act desperate.
Don't procrastinate —
　　there's no time to lose.
Run like a deer from the hunter,
　　fly like a bird from the trapper!

A LESSON FROM THE ANT

6-11　You lazy fool, look at an ant.
　　Watch it closely; let it teach you a thing or two.
Nobody has to tell it what to do.
　　All summer it stores up food;
　　at harvest it stockpiles provisions.
So how long are you going to laze around doing nothing?
　　How long before you get out of bed?
A nap here, a nap there, a day off here, a day off there,
　　sit back, take it easy — do you know what comes next?
Just this: You can look forward to a dirt-poor life,
　　poverty your permanent houseguest!

ALWAYS COOKING UP SOMETHING NASTY

12-15　Riffraff and rascals
　　talk out of both sides of their mouths.
They wink at each other, they shuffle their feet,
　　they cross their fingers behind their backs.
Their perverse minds are always cooking up something nasty,
　　always stirring up trouble.
Catastrophe is just around the corner for them,
　　a total smashup, their lives ruined beyond repair.

SEVEN THINGS GOD HATES

16-19　Here are six things GOD hates,
　　and one more that he loathes with a passion:

eyes that are arrogant,
a tongue that lies,
hands that murder the innocent,
a heart that hatches evil plots,
feet that race down a wicked track,
a mouth that lies under oath,
a troublemaker in the family.

WARNING ON ADULTERY

20-23   Good friend, follow your father's good advice;
don't wander off from your mother's teachings.
Wrap yourself in them from head to foot;
wear them like a scarf around your neck.
Wherever you walk, they'll guide you;
whenever you rest, they'll guard you;
when you wake up, they'll tell you what's next.
For sound advice is a beacon,
good teaching is a light,
moral discipline is a life path.

24-35   They'll protect you from wanton women,
from the seductive talk of some temptress.
Don't lustfully fantasize on her beauty,
nor be taken in by her bedroom eyes.
You can buy an hour with a whore for a loaf of bread,
but a wanton woman may well eat *you* alive.
Can you build a fire in your lap
and not burn your pants?
Can you walk barefoot on hot coals
and not get blisters?
It's the same when you have sex with your neighbor's wife:
Touch her and you'll pay for it. No excuses.
Hunger is no excuse
for a thief to steal;
When he's caught he has to pay it back,
even if he has to put his whole house in hock.
·   Adultery is a brainless act,
soul-destroying, self-destructive;
Expect a bloody nose, a black eye,
and a reputation ruined for good.
For jealousy detonates rage in a cheated husband;
wild for revenge, he won't make allowances.

Nothing you say or pay will make it all right;
neither bribes nor reason will satisfy him.

DRESSED TO SEDUCE

1-5   **7** Dear friend, do what I tell you;
treasure my careful instructions.
Do what I say and you'll live well.
My teaching is as precious as your eyesight — guard it!
Write it out on the back of your hands;
etch it on the chambers of your heart.
Talk to Wisdom as to a sister.
Treat Insight as your companion.
They'll be with you to fend off the Temptress —
that smooth-talking, honey-tongued Seductress.

6-12   As I stood at the window of my house
looking out through the shutters,
Watching the mindless crowd stroll by,
I spotted a young man without any sense
Arriving at the corner of the street where she lived,
then turning up the path to her house.
It was dusk, the evening coming on,
the darkness thickening into night.
Just then, a woman met him —
she'd been lying in wait for him, dressed to seduce him.
Brazen and brash she was,
restless and roaming, never at home,
Walking the streets, loitering in the mall,
hanging out at every corner in town.

13-20   She threw her arms around him and kissed him,
boldly took his arm and said,
"I've got all the makings for a feast —
today I made my offerings, my vows are all paid,
So now I've come to find you,
hoping to catch sight of your face — and here you are!
I've spread fresh, clean sheets on my bed,
colorful imported linens.
My bed is aromatic with spices
and exotic fragrances.
Come, let's make love all night,
spend the night in ecstatic lovemaking!

My husband's not home; he's away on business,
and he won't be back for a month."

21-23   Soon she has him eating out of her hand,
bewitched by her honeyed speech.
Before you know it, he's trotting behind her,
like a calf led to the butcher shop,
Like a stag lured into ambush
and then shot with an arrow,
Like a bird flying into a net
not knowing that its flying life is over.

24-27   So, friends, listen to me,
take these words of mine most seriously.
Don't fool around with a woman like that;
don't even stroll through her neighborhood.
Countless victims come under her spell;
she's the death of many a poor man.
She runs a halfway house to hell,
fits you out with a shroud and a coffin.

LADY WISDOM CALLS OUT

1-11   8 Do you hear Lady Wisdom calling?
Can you hear Madame Insight raising her voice?
She's taken her stand at First and Main,
at the busiest intersection.
Right in the city square
where the traffic is thickest, she shouts,
"You — I'm talking to all of you,
everyone out here on the streets!
Listen, you idiots — learn good sense!
You blockheads — shape up!
Don't miss a word of this — I'm telling you how to live well,
I'm telling you how to live at your best.
My mouth chews and savors and relishes truth —
I can't stand the taste of evil!
You'll only hear true and right words from my mouth;
not one syllable will be twisted or skewed.
You'll recognize this as true — you with open minds;
truth-ready minds will see it at once.
Prefer my life-disciplines over chasing after money,
and God-knowledge over a lucrative career.

For Wisdom is better than all the trappings of wealth;
  nothing you could wish for holds a candle to her.

12-21 "I am Lady Wisdom, and I live next to Sanity;
  Knowledge and Discretion live just down the street.
The Fear-of-GOD means hating Evil,
  whose ways I hate with a passion —
  pride and arrogance and crooked talk.
Good counsel and common sense are my characteristics;
  I am both Insight and the Virtue to live it out.
With my help, leaders rule,
  and lawmakers legislate fairly;
With my help, governors govern,
  along with all in legitimate authority.
I love those who love me;
  those who look for me find me.
Wealth and Glory accompany me —
  also substantial Honor and a Good Name.
My benefits are worth more than a big salary, even a *very* big salary;
  the returns on me exceed any imaginable bonus.
You can find me on Righteous Road — that's where I walk —
  at the intersection of Justice Avenue,
Handing out life to those who love me,
  filling their arms with life — armloads of life!

22-31 "GOD sovereignly made me — the first, the basic —
  before he did anything else.
I was brought into being a long time ago,
  well before Earth got its start.
I arrived on the scene before Ocean,
  yes, even before Springs and Rivers and Lakes.
Before Mountains were sculpted and Hills took shape,
  I was already there, newborn;
Long before GOD stretched out Earth's Horizons,
  and tended to the minute details of Soil and Weather,
And set Sky firmly in place,
  I was there.
When he mapped and gave borders to wild Ocean,
  built the vast vault of Heaven,
  and installed the fountains that fed Ocean,
When he drew a boundary for Sea,
  posted a sign that said NO TRESPASSING,

And then staked out Earth's Foundations,
　　I was right there with him, making sure everything fit.
Day after day I was there, with my joyful applause,
　　always enjoying his company,
Delighted with the world of things and creatures,
　　happily celebrating the human family.

32-36　"So, my dear friends, listen carefully;
　　those who embrace these my ways are most blessed.
Mark a life of discipline and live wisely;
　　don't squander your precious life.
Blessed the man, blessed the woman, who listens to me,
　　awake and ready for me each morning,
　　alert and responsive as I start my day's work.
When you find me, you find life, real life,
　　to say nothing of GOD's good pleasure.
But if you wrong me, you damage your very soul;
　　when you reject me, you're flirting with death."

LADY WISDOM GIVES A DINNER PARTY

1-6　9 Lady Wisdom has built and furnished her home;
　　it's supported by seven hewn timbers.
　　The banquet meal is ready to be served: lamb roasted,
　　wine poured out, table set with silver and flowers.
Having dismissed her serving maids,
　　Lady Wisdom goes to town, stands in a prominent place,
　　and invites everyone within sound of her voice:
"Are you confused about life, don't know what's going on?
　　Come with me, oh come, have dinner with me!
I've prepared a wonderful spread — fresh-baked bread,
　　roast lamb, carefully selected wines.
Leave your impoverished confusion and *live*!
　　Walk up the street to a life with meaning."

7-12　If you reason with an arrogant cynic, you'll get slapped in the face;
　　confront bad behavior and get a kick in the shins.
So don't waste your time on a scoffer;
　　all you'll get for your pains is abuse.
But if you correct those who care about life,
　　that's different — they'll love you for it!
Save your breath for the wise — they'll be wiser for it;

tell good people what you know — they'll profit from it.
Skilled living gets its start in the Fear-of-GOD,
    insight into life from knowing a Holy God.
It's through me, Lady Wisdom, that your life deepens,
    and the years of your life ripen.
Live wisely and wisdom will permeate your life;
    mock life and life will mock you.

MADAME WHORE CALLS OUT, TOO

13-18   Then there's this other woman, Madame Whore —
    brazen, empty-headed, frivolous.
She sits on the front porch
    of her house on Main Street,
And as people walk by minding
    their own business, calls out,
"Are you confused about life, don't know what's going on?
    Steal off with me, I'll show you a good time!
    No one will ever know — I'll give you the time of your life."
But they don't know about all the skeletons in her closet,
    that all her guests end up in hell.

THE WISE SAYINGS OF SOLOMON
AN HONEST LIFE IS IMMORTAL

1   **10** Wise son, glad father;
      stupid son, sad mother.

2   Ill-gotten gain gets you nowhere;
    an honest life is immortal.

3   GOD won't starve an honest soul,
    but he frustrates the appetites of the wicked.

4   Sloth makes you poor;
    diligence brings wealth.

5   Make hay while the sun shines — that's smart;
    go fishing during harvest — that's stupid.

6   Blessings accrue on a good and honest life,
    but the mouth of the wicked is a dark cave of abuse.

7   A good and honest life is a blessed memorial;
    a wicked life leaves a rotten stench.

8   A wise heart takes orders;
     an empty head will come unglued.

9   Honesty lives confident and carefree,
     but Shifty is sure to be exposed.

10   An evasive eye is a sign of trouble ahead,
      but an open, face-to-face meeting results in peace.

11   The mouth of a good person is a deep, life-giving well,
      but the mouth of the wicked is a dark cave of abuse.

12   Hatred starts fights,
      but love pulls a quilt over the bickering.

13   You'll find wisdom on the lips of a person of insight,
      but the shortsighted needs a slap in the face.

14   The wise accumulate knowledge — a true treasure;
      know-it-alls talk too much — a sheer waste.

THE ROAD TO LIFE IS A DISCIPLINED LIFE

15   The wealth of the rich is their bastion;
      the poverty of the indigent is their ruin.

16   The wage of a good person is exuberant life;
      an evil person ends up with nothing but sin.

17   The road to life is a disciplined life;
      ignore correction and you're lost for good.

18   Liars secretly hoard hatred;
      fools openly spread slander.

19   The more talk, the less truth;
      the wise measure their words.

20   The speech of a good person is worth waiting for;
      the blabber of the wicked is worthless.

21   The talk of a good person is rich fare for many,
      but chatterboxes die of an empty heart.

FEAR-OF-GOD EXPANDS YOUR LIFE

22   GOD's blessing makes life rich;
     nothing we do can improve on God.

23   An empty-head thinks mischief is fun,
     but a mindful person relishes wisdom.

24   The nightmares of the wicked come true;
     what the good people desire, they get.

25   When the storm is over, there's nothing left of the wicked;
     good people, firm on their rock foundation, aren't even fazed.

26   A lazy employee will give you nothing but trouble;
     it's vinegar in the mouth, smoke in the eyes.

27   The Fear-of-GOD expands your life;
     a wicked life is a puny life.

28   The aspirations of good people end in celebration;
     the ambitions of bad people crash.

29   GOD is solid backing to a well-lived life,
     but he calls into question a shabby performance.

30   Good people *last* — they can't be moved;
     the wicked are here today, gone tomorrow.

31   A good person's mouth is a clear fountain of wisdom;
     a foul mouth is a stagnant swamp.

32   The speech of a good person clears the air;
     the words of the wicked pollute it.

WITHOUT GOOD DIRECTION, PEOPLE LOSE THEIR WAY

1   **11** GOD hates cheating in the marketplace;
     he loves it when business is aboveboard.

2   The stuck-up fall flat on their faces,
     but down-to-earth people stand firm.

3   The integrity of the honest keeps them on track;
     the deviousness of crooks brings them to ruin.

4   A thick bankroll is no help when life falls apart,
        but a principled life can stand up to the worst.

5   Moral character makes for smooth traveling;
        an evil life is a hard life.

6   Good character is the best insurance;
        crooks get trapped in their sinful lust.

7   When the wicked die, that's it —
        the story's over, end of hope.

8   A good person is saved from much trouble;
        a bad person runs straight into it.

9   The loose tongue of the godless spreads destruction;
        the common sense of the godly preserves them.

10   When it goes well for good people, the whole town cheers;
        when it goes badly for bad people, the town celebrates.

11   When right-living people bless the city, it flourishes;
        evil talk turns it into a ghost town in no time.

12   Mean-spirited slander is heartless;
        quiet discretion accompanies good sense.

13   A gadabout gossip can't be trusted with a secret,
        but someone of integrity won't violate a confidence.

14   Without good direction, people lose their way;
        the more wise counsel you follow, the better your chances.

15   Whoever makes deals with strangers is sure to get burned;
        if you keep a cool head, you'll avoid rash bargains.

16   A woman of gentle grace gets respect,
        but men of rough violence grab for loot.

A GOD-SHAPED LIFE

17   When you're kind to others, you help yourself;
        when you're cruel to others, you hurt yourself.

18   Bad work gets paid with a bad check;
      good work gets solid pay.

19   Take your stand with God's loyal community and live,
      or chase after phantoms of evil and die.

20   GOD can't stand deceivers,
      but oh how he relishes integrity.

21   Count on this: The wicked won't get off scot-free,
      and God's loyal people will triumph.

22   Like a gold ring in a pig's snout
      is a beautiful face on an empty head.

23   The desires of good people lead straight to the best,
      but wicked ambition ends in angry frustration.

24   The world of the generous gets larger and larger;
      the world of the stingy gets smaller and smaller.

25   The one who blesses others is abundantly blessed;
      those who help others are helped.

26   Curses on those who drive a hard bargain!
      Blessings on all who play fair and square!

27   The one who seeks good finds delight;
      the student of evil becomes evil.

28   A life devoted to things is a dead life, a stump;
      a God-shaped life is a flourishing tree.

29   Exploit or abuse your family, and end up with a fistful of air;
      common sense tells you it's a stupid way to live.

30   A good life is a fruit-bearing tree;
      a violent life destroys souls.

31   If good people barely make it,
      what's in store for the bad!

IF YOU LOVE LEARNING

1 12 If you love learning, you love the discipline that goes with it —
how shortsighted to refuse correction!

2 A good person basks in the delight of GOD,
and he wants nothing to do with devious schemers.

3 You can't find firm footing in a swamp,
but life rooted in God stands firm.

4 A hearty wife invigorates her husband,
but a frigid woman is cancer in the bones.

5 The thinking of principled people makes for justice;
the plots of degenerates corrupt.

6 The words of the wicked kill;
the speech of the upright saves.

7 Wicked people fall to pieces — there's nothing to them;
the homes of good people hold together.

8 A person who talks sense is honored;
airheads are held in contempt.

9 Better to be ordinary and work for a living
than act important and starve in the process.

10 Good people are good to their animals;
the "good-hearted" bad people kick and abuse them.

11 The one who stays on the job has food on the table;
the witless chase whims and fancies.

12 What the wicked construct finally falls into ruin,
while the roots of the righteous give life, and more life.

WISE PEOPLE TAKE ADVICE

13 The gossip of bad people gets them in trouble;
the conversation of good people keeps them out of it.

14   Well-spoken words bring satisfaction;
          well-done work has its own reward.

15   Fools are headstrong and do what they like;
          wise people take advice.

16   Fools have short fuses and explode all too quickly;
          the prudent quietly shrug off insults.

17   Truthful witness by a good person clears the air,
          but liars lay down a smoke screen of deceit.

18   Rash language cuts and maims,
          but there is healing in the words of the wise.

19   Truth lasts;
          lies are here today, gone tomorrow.

20   Evil scheming distorts the schemer;
          peace-planning brings joy to the planner.

21   No evil can overwhelm a good person,
          but the wicked have their hands full of it.

22   God can't stomach liars;
          he loves the company of those who keep their word.

23   Prudent people don't flaunt their knowledge;
          talkative fools broadcast their silliness.

24   The diligent find freedom in their work;
          the lazy are oppressed by work.

25   Worry weighs us down;
          a cheerful word picks us up.

26   A good person survives misfortune,
          but a wicked life invites disaster.

27   A lazy life is an empty life,
          but "early to rise" gets the job done.

28   Good men and women travel right into life;
     sin's detours take you straight to hell.

WALK WITH THE WISE

1   **13** Intelligent children listen to their parents;
     foolish children do their own thing.

2   The good acquire a taste for helpful conversation;
     bullies push and shove their way through life.

3   Careful words make for a careful life;
     careless talk may ruin everything.

4   Indolence wants it all and gets nothing;
     the energetic have something to show for their lives.

5   A good person hates false talk;
     a bad person wallows in gibberish.

6   A God-loyal life keeps you on track;
     sin dumps the wicked in the ditch.

7   A pretentious, showy life is an empty life;
     a plain and simple life is a full life.

8   The rich can be sued for everything they have,
     but the poor are free of such threats.

9   The lives of good people are brightly lit streets;
     the lives of the wicked are dark alleys.

10   Arrogant know-it-alls stir up discord,
     but wise men and women listen to each other's counsel.

11   Easy come, easy go,
     but steady diligence pays off.

12   Unrelenting disappointment leaves you heartsick,
     but a sudden good break can turn life around.

13   Ignore the Word and suffer;
     honor God's commands and grow rich.

14   The teaching of the wise is a fountain of life,
          so, no more drinking from death-tainted wells!

15   Sound thinking makes for gracious living,
          but liars walk a rough road.

16   A commonsense person *lives* good sense;
          fools litter the country with silliness.

17   Irresponsible talk makes a real mess of things,
          but a reliable reporter is a healing presence.

18   Refuse discipline and end up homeless;
          embrace correction and live an honored life.

19   Souls who follow their hearts thrive;
          fools bent on evil despise matters of soul.

20   Become wise by walking with the wise;
          hang out with fools and watch your life fall to pieces.

21   Disaster entraps sinners,
          but God-loyal people get a good life.

22   A good life gets passed on to the grandchildren;
          ill-gotten wealth ends up with good people.

23   Banks foreclose on the farms of the poor,
          or else the poor lose their shirts to crooked lawyers.

24   A refusal to correct is a refusal to love;
          love your children by disciplining them.

25   An appetite for good brings much satisfaction,
          but the belly of the wicked always wants more.

A WAY THAT LEADS TO HELL

1   **14** Lady Wisdom builds a lovely home;
          Sir Fool comes along and tears it down brick by brick.

2   An honest life shows respect for GOD;
          a degenerate life is a slap in his face.

3 Frivolous talk provokes a derisive smile;
    wise speech evokes nothing but respect.

4 No cattle, no crops;
    a good harvest requires a strong ox for the plow.

5 A true witness never lies;
    a false witness makes a business of it.

6 Cynics look high and low for wisdom — and never find it;
    the open-minded find it right on their doorstep!

7 Escape quickly from the company of fools;
    they're a waste of your time, a waste of your words.

8 The wisdom of the wise keeps life on track;
    the foolishness of fools lands them in the ditch.

9 The stupid ridicule right and wrong,
    but a moral life is a favored life.

10 The person who shuns the bitter moments of friends
    will be an outsider at their celebrations.

11 Lives of careless wrongdoing are tumbledown shacks;
    holy living builds soaring cathedrals.

12-13 There's a way of life that looks harmless enough;
    look again — it leads straight to hell.
    Sure, those people appear to be having a good time,
    but all that laughter will end in heartbreak.

SIFT AND WEIGH EVERY WORD

14 A mean person gets paid back in meanness,
    a gracious person in grace.

15 The gullible believe anything they're told;
    the prudent sift and weigh every word.

16 The wise watch their steps and avoid evil;
    fools are headstrong and reckless.

17   The hotheaded do things they'll later regret;
        the coldhearted get the cold shoulder.

18   Foolish dreamers live in a world of illusion;
        wise realists plant their feet on the ground.

19   Eventually, evil will pay tribute to good;
        the wicked will respect God-loyal people.

20   An unlucky loser is shunned by all,
        but everyone loves a winner.

21   It's criminal to ignore a neighbor in need,
        but compassion for the poor — what a blessing!

22   Isn't it obvious that conspirators lose out,
        while the thoughtful win love and trust?

23   Hard work always pays off;
        mere talk puts no bread on the table.

24   The wise accumulate wisdom;
        fools get stupider by the day.

25   Souls are saved by truthful witness
        and betrayed by the spread of lies.

26   The Fear-of-GOD builds up confidence,
        and makes a world safe for your children.

27   The Fear-of-GOD is a spring of living water
        so you won't go off drinking from poisoned wells.

28   The mark of a good leader is loyal followers;
        leadership is nothing without a following.

29   Slowness to anger makes for deep understanding;
        a quick-tempered person stockpiles stupidity.

30   A sound mind makes for a robust body,
        but runaway emotions corrode the bones.

31   You insult your Maker when you exploit the powerless;
       when you're kind to the poor, you honor God.

32   The evil of bad people leaves them out in the cold;
       the integrity of good people creates a safe place for living.

33   Lady Wisdom is at home in an understanding heart —
       fools never even get to say hello.

34   God-devotion makes a country strong;
       God-avoidance leaves people weak.

35   Diligent work gets a warm commendation;
       shiftless work earns an angry rebuke.

GOD DOESN'T MISS A THING

1   **15** A gentle response defuses anger,
             but a sharp tongue kindles a temper-fire.

2   Knowledge flows like spring water from the wise;
      fools are leaky faucets, dripping nonsense.

3   GOD doesn't miss a thing —
      he's alert to good and evil alike.

4   Kind words heal and help;
      cutting words wound and maim.

5   Moral dropouts won't listen to their elders;
      welcoming correction is a mark of good sense.

6   The lives of God-loyal people flourish;
      a misspent life is soon bankrupt.

7   Perceptive words spread knowledge;
      fools are hollow — there's nothing to them.

8   GOD can't stand pious poses,
      but he delights in genuine prayers.

9   A life frittered away disgusts GOD;
      he loves those who run straight for the finish line.

10 It's a school of hard knocks for those who leave God's path,
      a dead-end street for those who hate God's rules.

11 Even hell holds no secrets from GOD —
      do you think he can't read human hearts?

Life Ascends to the Heights

12 Know-it-alls don't like being told what to do;
      they avoid the company of wise men and women.

13 A cheerful heart brings a smile to your face;
      a sad heart makes it hard to get through the day.

14 An intelligent person is always eager to take in more truth;
      fools feed on fast-food fads and fancies.

15 A miserable heart means a miserable life;
      a cheerful heart fills the day with song.

16 A simple life in the Fear-of-GOD
      is better than a rich life with a ton of headaches.

17 Better a bread crust shared in love
      than a slab of prime rib served in hate.

18 Hot tempers start fights;
      a calm, cool spirit keeps the peace.

19 The path of lazy people is overgrown with briers;
      the diligent walk down a smooth road.

20 Intelligent children make their parents proud;
      lazy students embarrass their parents.

21 The empty-headed treat life as a plaything;
      the perceptive grasp its meaning and make a go of it.

22 Refuse good advice and watch your plans fail;
      take good counsel and watch them succeed.

23 Congenial conversation — what a pleasure!
      The right word at the right time — beautiful!

24   Life ascends to the heights for the thoughtful —
     it's a clean about-face from descent into hell.

25   GOD smashes the pretensions of the arrogant;
     he stands with those who have no standing.

26   GOD can't stand evil scheming,
     but he puts words of grace and beauty on display.

27   A greedy and grasping person destroys community;
     those who refuse to exploit live and let live.

28   Prayerful answers come from God-loyal people;
     the wicked are sewers of abuse.

29   GOD keeps his distance from the wicked;
     he closely attends to the prayers of God-loyal people.

30   A twinkle in the eye means joy in the heart,
     and good news makes you feel fit as a fiddle.

31   Listen to good advice if you want to live well,
     an honored guest among wise men and women.

32   An undisciplined, self-willed life is puny;
     an obedient, God-willed life is spacious.

33   Fear-of-GOD is a school in skilled living —
     first you learn humility, then you experience glory.

EVERYTHING WITH A PLACE AND A PURPOSE

1   **16** Mortals make elaborate plans,
     but GOD has the last word.

2   Humans are satisfied with whatever looks good;
     GOD probes for what *is* good.

3   Put GOD in charge of your work,
     then what you've planned will take place.

4   GOD made everything with a place and purpose;
     even the wicked are included — but for *judgment*.

5   GOD can't stomach arrogance or pretense;
        believe me, he'll put those upstarts in their place.

6   Guilt is banished through love and truth;
        Fear-of-GOD deflects evil.

7   When GOD approves of your life,
        even your enemies will end up shaking your hand.

8   Far better to be right and poor
        than to be wrong and rich.

9   We plan the way we want to live,
        but only GOD makes us able to live it.

IT PAYS TO TAKE LIFE SERIOUSLY

10 A good leader motivates,
        doesn't mislead, doesn't exploit.

11 GOD cares about honesty in the workplace;
        your business is his business.

12 Good leaders abhor wrongdoing of all kinds;
        sound leadership has a moral foundation.

13 Good leaders cultivate honest speech;
        they love advisors who tell them the truth.

14 An intemperate leader wreaks havoc in lives;
        you're smart to stay clear of someone like that.

15 Good-tempered leaders invigorate lives;
        they're like spring rain and sunshine.

16 Get wisdom — it's worth more than money;
        choose insight over income every time.

17 The road of right living bypasses evil;
        watch your step and save your life.

18 First pride, then the crash —
        the bigger the ego, the harder the fall.

19   It's better to live humbly among the poor
         than to live it up among the rich and famous.

20   It pays to take life seriously;
         things work out when you trust in GOD.

21   A wise person gets known for insight;
         gracious words add to one's reputation.

22   True intelligence is a spring of fresh water,
         while fools sweat it out the hard way.

23   They make a lot of sense, these wise folks;
         whenever they speak, their reputation increases.

24   Gracious speech is like clover honey —
         good taste to the soul, quick energy for the body.

25   There's a way that looks harmless enough;
         look again — it leads straight to hell.

26   Appetite is an incentive to work;
         hunger makes you work all the harder.

27   Mean people spread mean gossip;
         their words smart and burn.

28   Troublemakers start fights;
         gossips break up friendships.

29   Calloused climbers betray their very own friends;
         they'd stab their own grandmothers in the back.

30   A shifty eye betrays an evil intention;
         a clenched jaw signals trouble ahead.

31   Gray hair is a mark of distinction,
         the award for a God-loyal life.

32   Moderation is better than muscle,
         self-control better than political power.

33   Make your motions and cast your votes,
        but GOD has the final say.

A WHACK ON THE HEAD OF A FOOL

1   **17** A meal of bread and water in contented peace
            is better than a banquet spiced with quarrels.

2   A wise servant takes charge of an unruly child
        and is honored as one of the family.

3   As silver in a crucible and gold in a pan,
        so our lives are assayed by GOD.

4   Evil people relish malicious conversation;
        the ears of liars itch for dirty gossip.

5   Whoever mocks poor people insults their Creator;
        gloating over misfortune is a punishable crime.

6   Old people are distinguished by grandchildren;
        children take pride in their parents.

7   We don't expect eloquence from fools,
        nor do we expect lies from our leaders.

8   Receiving a gift is like getting a rare gemstone;
        any way you look at it, you see beauty refracted.

9   Overlook an offense and bond a friendship;
        fasten on to a slight and — good-bye, friend!

10   A quiet rebuke to a person of good sense
        does more than a whack on the head of a fool.

11   Criminals out looking for nothing but trouble
        won't have to wait long — they'll meet it coming and going!

12   Better to meet a grizzly robbed of her cubs
        than a fool hellbent on folly.

13   Those who return evil for good
        will meet their own evil returning.

14   The start of a quarrel is like a leak in a dam,
         so stop it before it bursts.

15   Whitewashing bad people and throwing mud on good people
         are equally abhorrent to GOD.

16   What's this? Fools out shopping for wisdom!
         They wouldn't recognize it if they saw it!

ONE WHO KNOWS MUCH SAYS LITTLE

17   Friends love through all kinds of weather,
         and families stick together in all kinds of trouble.

18   It's stupid to try to get something for nothing,
         or run up huge bills you can never pay.

19   The person who courts sin marries trouble;
         build a wall, invite a burglar.

20   A bad motive can't achieve a good end;
         double-talk brings you double trouble.

21   Having a fool for a child is misery;
         it's no fun being the parent of a dolt.

22   A cheerful disposition is good for your health;
         gloom and doom leave you bone-tired.

23   The wicked take bribes under the table;
         they show nothing but contempt for justice.

24   The perceptive find wisdom in their own front yard;
         fools look for it everywhere but right here.

25   A surly, stupid child is sheer pain to a father,
         a bitter pill for a mother to swallow.

26   It's wrong to penalize good behavior,
         or make good citizens pay for the crimes of others.

27   The one who knows much says little;
         an understanding person remains calm.

28 Even dunces who keep quiet are thought to be wise;
      as long as they keep their mouths shut, they're smart.

WORDS KILL, WORDS GIVE LIFE

1 **18** Loners who care only for themselves
              spit on the common good.

2 Fools care nothing for thoughtful discourse;
      all they do is run off at the mouth.

3 When wickedness arrives, shame's not far behind;
      contempt for life is contemptible.

4 Many words rush along like rivers in flood,
      but deep wisdom flows up from artesian springs.

5 It's not right to go easy on the guilty,
      or come down hard on the innocent.

6 The words of a fool start fights;
      do him a favor and gag him.

7 Fools are undone by their big mouths;
      their souls are crushed by their words.

8 Listening to gossip is like eating cheap candy;
      do you really want junk like that in your belly?

9 Slack habits and sloppy work
      are as bad as vandalism.

10 GOD's name is a place of protection —
      good people can run there and be safe.

11 The rich think their wealth protects them;
      they imagine themselves safe behind it.

12 Pride first, then the crash,
      but humility is precursor to honor.

13 Answering before listening
      is both stupid and rude.

14   A healthy spirit conquers adversity,
         but what can you do when the spirit is crushed?

15   Wise men and women are always learning,
         always listening for fresh insights.

16   A gift gets attention;
         it buys the attention of eminent people.

17   The first speech in a court case is always convincing —
         until the cross-examination starts!

18   You may have to draw straws
         when faced with a tough decision.

19   Do a favor and win a friend forever;
         nothing can untie that bond.

20   Words satisfy the mind as much as fruit does the stomach;
         good talk is as gratifying as a good harvest.

21   Words kill, words give life;
         they're either poison or fruit — you choose.

22   Find a good spouse, you find a good life —
         and even more: the favor of GOD!

23   The poor speak in soft supplications;
         the rich bark out answers.

24   Friends come and friends go,
         but a true friend sticks by you like family.

IF YOU QUIT LISTENING

1   **19** Better to be poor and honest
            than a rich person no one can trust.

2   Ignorant zeal is worthless;
         haste makes waste.

3   People ruin their lives by their own stupidity,
         so why does GOD always get blamed?

4   Wealth attracts friends as honey draws flies,
      but poor people are avoided like a plague.

5   Perjury won't go unpunished.
      Would you let a liar go free?

6   Lots of people flock around a generous person;
      everyone's a friend to the philanthropist.

7   When you're down on your luck, even your family avoids you —
      yes, even your best friends wish you'd get lost.
   If they see you coming, they look the other way —
      out of sight, out of mind.

8   Grow a wise heart — you'll do yourself a favor;
      keep a clear head — you'll find a good life.

9   The person who tells lies gets caught;
      the person who spreads rumors is ruined.

10 Blockheads shouldn't live on easy street
      any more than workers should give orders to their boss.

11 Smart people know how to hold their tongue;
      their grandeur is to forgive and forget.

12 Mean-tempered leaders are like mad dogs;
      the good-natured are like fresh morning dew.

13 A parent is worn to a frazzle by a stupid child;
      a nagging spouse is a leaky faucet.

14 House and land are handed down from parents,
      but a congenial spouse comes straight from GOD.

15 Life collapses on loafers;
      lazybones go hungry.

16 Keep the rules and keep your life;
      careless living kills.

17 Mercy to the needy is a loan to GOD,
      and GOD pays back those loans in full.

18   Discipline your children while you still have the chance;
          indulging them destroys them.

19   Let angry people endure the backlash of their own anger;
          if you try to make it better, you'll only make it worse.

20   Take good counsel and accept correction —
          that's the way to live wisely and well.

21   We humans keep brainstorming options and plans,
          but GOD's purpose prevails.

22   It's only human to want to make a buck,
          but it's better to be poor than a liar.

23   Fear-of-GOD is life itself,
          a full life, and serene — no nasty surprises.

24   Some people dig a fork into the pie
          but are too lazy to raise it to their mouth.

25   Punish the insolent — make an example of them.
          Who knows? Somebody might learn a good lesson.

26   Kids who lash out against their parents
          are an embarrassment and disgrace.

27   If you quit listening, dear child, and strike off on your own,
          you'll soon be out of your depth.

28   An unprincipled witness desecrates justice;
          the mouths of the wicked spew malice.

29   The irreverent have to learn reverence the hard way;
          only a slap in the face brings fools to attention.

DEEP WATER IN THE HEART

1   20 Wine makes you mean, beer makes you quarrelsome —
          a staggering drunk is not much fun.

2   Quick-tempered leaders are like mad dogs —
          cross them and they bite your head off.

3   It's a mark of good character to avert quarrels,
      but fools love to pick fights.

4   A farmer too lazy to plant in the spring
      has nothing to harvest in the fall.

5   Knowing what is right is like deep water in the heart;
      a wise person draws from the well within.

6   Lots of people claim to be loyal and loving,
      but where on earth can you find one?

7   God-loyal people, living honest lives,
      make it much easier for their children.

8-9   Leaders who know their business and care
      keep a sharp eye out for the shoddy and cheap,
    For who among us can be trusted
      to be always diligent and honest?

10   Switching price tags and padding the expense account
      are two things GOD hates.

11   Young people eventually reveal by their actions
      if their motives are on the up and up.

DRINKING FROM THE CHALICE OF KNOWLEDGE

12   Ears that hear and eyes that see —
      we get our basic equipment from GOD!

13   Don't be too fond of sleep; you'll end up in the poorhouse.
      Wake up and get up; then there'll be food on the table.

14   The shopper says, "That's junk — I'll take it off your hands,"
      then goes off boasting of the bargain.

15   Drinking from the beautiful chalice of knowledge
      is better than adorning oneself with gold and rare gems.

16   Hold tight to collateral on any loan to a stranger;
      beware of accepting what a transient has pawned.

17   Stolen bread tastes sweet,
          but soon your mouth is full of gravel.

18   Form your purpose by asking for counsel,
          then carry it out using all the help you can get.

19   Gossips can't keep secrets,
          so never confide in blabbermouths.

20   Anyone who curses father and mother
          extinguishes light and exists benighted.

THE VERY STEPS WE TAKE

21   A bonanza at the beginning
          is no guarantee of blessing at the end.

22   Don't ever say, "I'll get you for that!"
          Wait for GOD; he'll settle the score.

23   GOD hates cheating in the marketplace;
          rigged scales are an outrage.

24   The very steps we take come from GOD;
          otherwise how would we know where we're going?

25   An impulsive vow is a trap;
          later you'll wish you could get out of it.

26   After careful scrutiny, a wise leader
          makes a clean sweep of rebels and dolts.

27   GOD is in charge of human life,
          watching and examining us inside and out.

28   Love and truth form a good leader;
          sound leadership is founded on loving integrity.

29   Youth may be admired for vigor,
          but gray hair gives prestige to old age.

30   A good thrashing purges evil;
          punishment goes deep within us.

God Examines Our Motives

1   **21** Good leadership is a channel of water controlled by God;
he directs it to whatever ends he chooses.

2   We justify our actions by appearances;
God examines our motives.

3   Clean living before God and justice with our neighbors
mean far more to God than religious performance.

4   Arrogance and pride — distinguishing marks in the wicked —
are just plain sin.

5   Careful planning puts you ahead in the long run;
hurry and scurry puts you further behind.

6   Make it to the top by lying and cheating;
get paid with smoke and a promotion — to death!

7   The wicked get buried alive by their loot
because they refuse to use it to help others.

8   Mixed motives twist life into tangles;
pure motives take you straight down the road.

Do Your Best, Prepare for the Worst

9   Better to live alone in a tumbledown shack
than share a mansion with a nagging spouse.

10   Wicked souls love to make trouble;
they feel nothing for friends and neighbors.

11   Simpletons only learn the hard way,
but the wise learn by listening.

12   A God-loyal person will see right through the wicked
and undo the evil they've planned.

13   If you stop your ears to the cries of the poor,
your cries will go unheard, unanswered.

14   A quietly given gift soothes an irritable person;
a heartfelt present cools a hot temper.

15   Good people celebrate when justice triumphs,
      but for the workers of evil it's a bad day.

16   Whoever wanders off the straight and narrow
      ends up in a congregation of ghosts.

17   You're addicted to thrills? What an empty life!
      The pursuit of pleasure is never satisfied.

18   What a bad person plots against the good, boomerangs;
      the plotter gets it in the end.

19   Better to live in a tent in the wild
      than with a cross and petulant spouse.

20   Valuables are safe in a wise person's home;
      fools put it all out for yard sales.

21   Whoever goes hunting for what is right and kind
      finds life itself — *glorious* life!

22   One sage entered a whole city of armed soldiers —
      their trusted defenses fell to pieces!

23   Watch your words and hold your tongue;
      you'll save yourself a lot of grief.

24   You know their names — Brash, Impudent, Blasphemer —
      intemperate hotheads, every one.

25   Lazy people finally die of hunger
      because they won't get up and go to work.

26   Sinners are always wanting what they don't have;
      the God-loyal are always giving what they do have.

27   Religious performance by the wicked stinks;
      it's even worse when they use it to get ahead.

28   A lying witness is unconvincing;
      a person who speaks truth is respected.

29 Unscrupulous people fake it a lot;
    honest people are sure of their steps.

30 Nothing clever, nothing conceived, nothing contrived,
    can get the better of GOD.

31 Do your best, prepare for the worst —
    then trust GOD to bring victory.

THE CURE COMES THROUGH DISCIPLINE

1 **22** A sterling reputation is better than striking it rich;
    a gracious spirit is better than money in the bank.

2 The rich and the poor shake hands as equals —
    GOD made them both!

3 A prudent person sees trouble coming and ducks;
    a simpleton walks in blindly and is clobbered.

4 The payoff for meekness and Fear-of-GOD
    is plenty and honor and a satisfying life.

5 The perverse travel a dangerous road, potholed and mud-slick;
    if you know what's good for you, stay clear of it.

6 Point your kids in the right direction —
    when they're old they won't be lost.

7 The poor are always ruled over by the rich,
    so don't borrow and put yourself under their power.

8 Whoever sows sin reaps weeds,
    and bullying anger sputters into nothing.

9 Generous hands are blessed hands
    because they give bread to the poor.

10 Kick out the troublemakers and things will quiet down;
    you need a break from bickering and griping!

11 GOD loves the pure-hearted and well-spoken;
    good leaders also delight in their friendship.

12   GOD guards knowledge with a passion,
   but he'll have nothing to do with deception.

13   The loafer says, "There's a lion on the loose!
   If I go out I'll be eaten alive!"

14   The mouth of a whore is a bottomless pit;
   you'll fall in that pit if you're on the outs with GOD.

15   Young people are prone to foolishness and fads;
   the cure comes through tough-minded discipline.

16   Exploit the poor or glad-hand the rich — whichever,
   you'll end up the poorer for it.

THE THIRTY PRECEPTS OF THE SAGES
DON'T MOVE BACK THE BOUNDARY LINES

17-21   Listen carefully to my wisdom;
   take to heart what I can teach you.
   You'll treasure its sweetness deep within;
   you'll give it bold expression in your speech.
   To make sure your foundation is trust in GOD,
   I'm laying it all out right now just for you.
   I'm giving you thirty sterling principles —
   tested guidelines to live by.
   Believe me — these are truths that work,
   and will keep you accountable
   to those who sent you.

1

22-23   Don't walk on the poor just because they're poor,
   and don't use your position to crush the weak,
   Because GOD will come to their defense;
   the life you took, he'll take from you and give back to them.

2

24-25   Don't hang out with angry people;
   don't keep company with hotheads.
   Bad temper is contagious —
   don't get infected.

3

26-27 Don't gamble on the pot of gold at the end of the rainbow,
      hocking your house against a lucky chance.
   The time will come when you have to pay up;
      you'll be left with nothing but the shirt on your back.

4

28 Don't stealthily move back the boundary lines
      staked out long ago by your ancestors.

5

29 Observe people who are good at their work —
      skilled workers are always in demand and admired;
      they don't take a backseat to anyone.

RESTRAIN YOURSELF

6

1-3 23 When you go out to dinner with an influential person,
            mind your manners:
         Don't gobble your food,
      don't talk with your mouth full.
   And don't stuff yourself;
      bridle your appetite.

7

4-5 Don't wear yourself out trying to get rich;
      restrain yourself!
   Riches disappear in the blink of an eye;
      wealth sprouts wings
      and flies off into the wild blue yonder.

8

6-8 Don't accept a meal from a tightwad;
      don't expect anything special.
   He'll be as stingy with you as he is with himself;
      he'll say, "Eat! Drink!" but won't mean a word of it.
   His miserly serving will turn your stomach
      when you realize the meal's a sham.

9

9 Don't bother talking sense to fools;
      they'll only poke fun at your words.

10

10-11   Don't stealthily move back the boundary lines
  or cheat orphans out of their property,
For they have a powerful Advocate
  who will go to bat for them.

11

12   Give yourselves to disciplined instruction;
  open your ears to tested knowledge.

12

13-14   Don't be afraid to correct your young ones;
  a spanking won't kill them.
A good spanking, in fact, might save them
  from something worse than death.

13

15-16   Dear child, if you become wise,
  I'll be one happy parent.
My heart will dance and sing
  to the tuneful truth you'll speak.

14

17-18   Don't for a minute envy careless rebels;
  soak yourself in the Fear-of-GOD —
That's where your future lies.
  Then you won't be left with an armload of nothing.

15

19-21   Oh listen, dear child — become wise;
  point your life in the right direction.
Don't drink too much wine and get drunk;
  don't eat too much food and get fat.
Drunks and gluttons will end up on skid row,
  in a stupor and dressed in rags.

BUY WISDOM, EDUCATION, INSIGHT

16

22-25   Listen with respect to the father who raised you,
  and when your mother grows old, don't neglect her.
Buy truth — don't sell it for love or money;

buy wisdom, buy education, buy insight.
Parents rejoice when their children turn out well;
    wise children become proud parents.
So make your father happy!
    Make your mother proud!

17

26 Dear child, I want your full attention;
    please do what I show you.

27-28 A whore is a bottomless pit;
    a loose woman can get you in deep trouble fast.
She'll take you for all you've got;
    she's worse than a pack of thieves.

18

29-35 Who are the people who are always crying the blues?
    Who do you know who reeks of self-pity?
Who keeps getting beat up for no reason at all?
    Whose eyes are bleary and bloodshot?
It's those who spend the night with a bottle,
    for whom drinking is serious business.
Don't judge wine by its label,
    or its bouquet, or its full-bodied flavor.
Judge it rather by the hangover it leaves you with —
    the splitting headache, the queasy stomach.
Do you really prefer seeing double,
    with your speech all slurred,
Reeling and seasick,
    drunk as a sailor?
"They hit me," you'll say, "but it didn't hurt;
    they beat on me, but I didn't feel a thing.
When I'm sober enough to manage it,
    bring me another drink!"

INTELLIGENCE OUTRANKS MUSCLE

19

1-2 **24** Don't envy bad people;
        don't even want to be around them.
    All they think about is causing a disturbance;
    all they talk about is making trouble.

20

3-4 It takes wisdom to build a house,
    and understanding to set it on a firm foundation;
It takes knowledge to furnish its rooms
    with fine furniture and beautiful draperies.

21

5-6 It's better to be wise than strong;
    intelligence outranks muscle any day.
Strategic planning is the key to warfare;
    to win, you need a lot of good counsel.

22

7 Wise conversation is way over the head of fools;
    in a serious discussion they haven't a clue.

23

8-9 The person who's always cooking up some evil
    soon gets a reputation as prince of rogues.
Fools incubate sin;
    cynics desecrate beauty.

RESCUE THE PERISHING

24

10 If you fall to pieces in a crisis,
    there wasn't much to you in the first place.

25

11-12 Rescue the perishing;
    don't hesitate to step in and help.
If you say, "Hey, that's none of my business,"
    will that get you off the hook?
Someone is watching you closely, you know —
    Someone not impressed with weak excuses.

26

13-14 Eat honey, dear child — it's good for you —
    and delicacies that melt in your mouth.
Likewise knowledge,
    and wisdom for your soul —
Get that and your future's secured,
    your hope is on solid rock.

27

15-16   Don't interfere with good people's lives;
        don't try to get the best of them.
  No matter how many times you trip them up,
        God-loyal people don't stay down long;
  Soon they're up on their feet,
        while the wicked end up flat on their faces.

28

17-18   Don't laugh when your enemy falls;
        don't crow over his collapse.
  GOD might see, and become very provoked,
        and then take pity on his plight.

29

19-20   Don't bother your head with braggarts
        or wish you could succeed like the wicked.
  Those people have no future at all;
        they're headed down a dead-end street.

30

21-22   Fear GOD, dear child — respect your leaders;
        don't be defiant or mutinous.
  Without warning your life can turn upside down,
        and who knows how or when it might happen?

MORE SAYINGS OF THE WISE
AN HONEST ANSWER

23   It's wrong, very wrong,
        to go along with injustice.

24-25   Whoever whitewashes the wicked
        gets a black mark in the history books,
  But whoever exposes the wicked
        will be thanked and rewarded.

26   An honest answer
        is like a warm hug.

27   First plant your fields;
        then build your barn.

28-29   Don't talk about your neighbors behind their backs —
       no slander or gossip, please.
    Don't say to anyone, "I'll get back at you for what you did to me.
       I'll make you pay for what you did!"

30-34   One day I walked by the field of an old lazybones,
       and then passed the vineyard of a lout;
    They were overgrown with weeds,
       thick with thistles, all the fences broken down.
    I took a long look and pondered what I saw;
       the fields preached me a sermon and I listened:
    "A nap here, a nap there, a day off here, a day off there,
       sit back, take it easy — do you know what comes next?
    Just this: You can look forward to a dirt-poor life,
       with poverty as your permanent houseguest!"

FURTHER WISE SAYINGS OF SOLOMON
The Right Word at the Right Time

1   **25** There are also these proverbs of Solomon,
       collected by scribes of Hezekiah, king of Judah.

2   God delights in concealing things;
       scientists delight in discovering things.

3   Like the horizons for breadth and the ocean for depth,
       the understanding of a good leader is broad and deep.

4-5   Remove impurities from the silver
       and the silversmith can craft a fine chalice;
    Remove the wicked from leadership
       and authority will be credible and God-honoring.

6-7   Don't work yourself into the spotlight;
       don't push your way into the place of prominence.
    It's better to be promoted to a place of honor
       than face humiliation by being demoted.

8   Don't jump to conclusions — there may be
       a perfectly good explanation for what you just saw.

9-10   In the heat of an argument,
       don't betray confidences;

Word is sure to get around,
 and no one will trust you.

11-12 The right word at the right time
  is like a custom-made piece of jewelry,
 And a wise friend's timely reprimand
  is like a gold ring slipped on your finger.

13 Reliable friends who do what they say
  are like cool drinks in sweltering heat — refreshing!

14 Like billowing clouds that bring no rain
  is the person who talks big but never produces.

15 Patient persistence pierces through indifference;
  gentle speech breaks down rigid defenses.

A Person Without Self-Control

16-17 When you're given a box of candy, don't gulp it all down;
  eat too much chocolate and you'll make yourself sick;
 And when you find a friend, don't outwear your welcome;
  show up at all hours and he'll soon get fed up.

18 Anyone who tells lies against the neighbors
  in court or on the street is a loose cannon.

19 Trusting a double-crosser when you're in trouble
  is like biting down on an abscessed tooth.

20 Singing light songs to the heavyhearted
  is like pouring salt in their wounds.

21-22 If you see your enemy hungry, go buy him lunch;
  if he's thirsty, bring him a drink.
 Your generosity will surprise him with goodness,
  and God will look after you.

23 A north wind brings stormy weather,
  and a gossipy tongue stormy looks.

24 Better to live alone in a tumbledown shack
  than share a mansion with a nagging spouse.

25   Like a cool drink of water when you're worn out and weary
        is a letter from a long-lost friend.

26   A good person who gives in to a bad person
        is a muddied spring, a polluted well.

27   It's not smart to stuff yourself with sweets,
        nor is glory piled on glory good for you.

28   A person without self-control
        is like a house with its doors and windows knocked out.

FOOLS RECYCLE SILLINESS

1   **26** We no more give honors to fools
        than pray for snow in summer or rain during harvest.

2   You have as little to fear from an undeserved curse
        as from the dart of a wren or the swoop of a swallow.

3   A whip for the racehorse, a tiller for the sailboat —
        and a stick for the back of fools!

4   Don't respond to the stupidity of a fool;
        you'll only look foolish yourself.

5   Answer a fool in simple terms
        so he doesn't get a swelled head.

6   You're only asking for trouble
        when you send a message by a fool.

7   A proverb quoted by fools
        is limp as a wet noodle.

8   Putting a fool in a place of honor
        is like setting a mud brick on a marble column.

9   To ask a moron to quote a proverb
        is like putting a scalpel in the hands of a drunk.

10   Hire a fool or a drunk
        and you shoot yourself in the foot.

11 As a dog eats its own vomit,
     so fools recycle silliness.

12 See that man who thinks he's so smart?
     You can expect far more from a fool than from him.

13 Loafers say, "It's dangerous out there!
     Tigers are prowling the streets!"
     and then pull the covers back over their heads.

14 Just as a door turns on its hinges,
     so a lazybones turns back over in bed.

15 A shiftless sluggard puts his fork in the pie,
     but is too lazy to lift it to his mouth.

LIKE GLAZE ON CRACKED POTTERY

16 Dreamers fantasize their self-importance;
     they think they are smarter
     than a whole college faculty.

17 You grab a mad dog by the ears
     when you butt into a quarrel that's none of your business.

18-19 People who shrug off deliberate deceptions,
     saying, "I didn't mean it, I was only joking,"
     Are worse than careless campers
     who walk away from smoldering campfires.

20 When you run out of wood, the fire goes out;
     when the gossip ends, the quarrel dies down.

21 A quarrelsome person in a dispute
     is like kerosene thrown on a fire.

22 Listening to gossip is like eating cheap candy;
     do you want junk like that in your belly?

23 Smooth talk from an evil heart
     is like glaze on cracked pottery.

24-26 Your enemy shakes hands and greets you like an old friend,
     all the while conniving against you.

When he speaks warmly to you, don't believe him for a minute;
   he's just waiting for the chance to rip you off.
No matter how cunningly he conceals his malice,
   eventually his evil will be exposed in public.

27   Malice backfires;
    spite boomerangs.

28   Liars hate their victims;
    flatterers sabotage trust.

You Don't Know Tomorrow

1   **27** Don't brashly announce what you're going to do tomorrow;
    you don't know the first thing about tomorrow.

2   Don't call attention to yourself;
    let others do that for you.

3   Carrying a log across your shoulders
    while you're hefting a boulder with your arms
Is nothing compared to the burden
    of putting up with a fool.

4   We're blasted by anger and swamped by rage,
    but who can survive jealousy?

5   A spoken reprimand is better
    than approval that's never expressed.

6   The wounds from a lover are worth it;
    kisses from an enemy do you in.

7   When you've stuffed yourself, you refuse dessert;
    when you're starved, you could eat a horse.

8   People who won't settle down, wandering hither and yon,
    are like restless birds, flitting to and fro.

9   Just as lotions and fragrance give sensual delight,
    a sweet friendship refreshes the soul.

10   Don't leave your friends or your parents' friends
    and run home to your family when things get rough;

Better a nearby friend
　　than a distant family.

11　Become wise, dear child, and make me happy;
　　then nothing the world throws my way will upset me.

12　A prudent person sees trouble coming and ducks;
　　a simpleton walks in blindly and is clobbered.

13　Hold tight to collateral on any loan to a stranger;
　　be wary of accepting what a transient has pawned.

14　If you wake your friend in the early morning
　　by shouting "Rise and shine!"
　　It will sound to him
　　more like a curse than a blessing.

15-16　A nagging spouse is like
　　the drip, drip, drip of a leaky faucet;
　　You can't turn it off,
　　and you can't get away from it.

YOUR FACE MIRRORS YOUR HEART

17　You use steel to sharpen steel,
　　and one friend sharpens another.

18　If you care for your orchard, you'll enjoy its fruit;
　　if you honor your boss, you'll be honored.

19　Just as water mirrors your face,
　　so your face mirrors your heart.

20　Hell has a voracious appetite,
　　and lust just never quits.

21　The purity of silver and gold is tested
　　by putting them in the fire;
　　The purity of human hearts is tested
　　by giving them a little fame.

22　Pound on a fool all you like —
　　you can't pound out foolishness.

23-27   Know your sheep by name;
  carefully attend to your flocks;
(Don't take them for granted;
  possessions don't last forever, you know.)
And then, when the crops are in
  and the harvest is stored in the barns,
You can knit sweaters from lambs' wool,
  and sell your goats for a profit;
There will be plenty of milk and meat
  to last your family through the winter.

IF YOU DESERT GOD'S LAW

1   **28** The wicked are edgy with guilt, ready to run off
  even when no one's after them;
Honest people are relaxed and confident,
bold as lions.

2   When the country is in chaos,
  everybody has a plan to fix it —
But it takes a leader of real understanding
  to straighten things out.

3   The wicked who oppress the poor
  are like a hailstorm that beats down the harvest.

4   If you desert God's law, you're free to embrace depravity;
  if you love God's law, you fight for it tooth and nail.

5   Justice makes no sense to the evilminded;
  those who seek GOD know it inside and out.

6   It's better to be poor and direct
  than rich and crooked.

7   Practice God's law — get a reputation for wisdom;
  hang out with a loose crowd — embarrass your family.

8   Get as rich as you want
  through cheating and extortion,
But eventually some friend of the poor
  is going to give it all back to them.

9   God has no use for the prayers
     of the people who won't listen to him.

10   Lead good people down a wrong path
     and you'll come to a bad end;
     do good and you'll be rewarded for it.

11   The rich think they know it all,
     but the poor can see right through them.

12   When good people are promoted, everything is great,
     but when the bad are in charge, watch out!

13   You can't whitewash your sins and get by with it;
     you find mercy by admitting and leaving them.

14   A tenderhearted person lives a blessed life;
     a hardhearted person lives a hard life.

15   Lions roar and bears charge —
     and the wicked lord it over the poor.

16   Among leaders who lack insight, abuse abounds,
     but for one who hates corruption, the future is bright.

17   A murderer haunted by guilt
     is doomed — there's no helping him.

18   Walk straight — live well and be saved;
     a devious life is a doomed life.

Doing Great Harm in Seemingly Harmless Ways

19   Work your garden — you'll end up with plenty of food;
     play and party — you'll end up with an empty plate.

20   Committed and persistent work pays off;
     get-rich-quick schemes are ripoffs.

21   Playing favorites is always a bad thing;
     you can do great harm in seemingly harmless ways.

22   A miser in a hurry to get rich
     doesn't know that he'll end up broke.

23   In the end, serious reprimand is appreciated
        far more than bootlicking flattery.

24   Anyone who robs father and mother
        and says, "So, what's wrong with that?"
        is worse than a pirate.

25   A grasping person stirs up trouble,
        but trust in GOD brings a sense of well-being.

26   If you think you know it all, you're a fool for sure;
        real survivors learn wisdom from others.

27   Be generous to the poor — you'll never go hungry;
        shut your eyes to their needs, and run a gauntlet of curses.

28   When corruption takes over, good people go underground,
        but when the crooks are thrown out, it's safe to come out.

IF PEOPLE CAN'T SEE WHAT GOD IS DOING

1   **29** For people who hate discipline
            and only get more stubborn,
            There'll come a day when life tumbles in and they break,
        but by then it'll be too late to help them.

2   When good people run things, everyone is glad,
        but when the ruler is bad, everyone groans.

3   If you love wisdom, you'll delight your parents,
        but you'll destroy their trust if you run with whores.

4   A leader of good judgment gives stability;
        an exploiting leader leaves a trail of waste.

5   A flattering neighbor is up to no good;
        he's probably planning to take advantage of you.

6   Evil people fall into their own traps;
        good people run the other way, glad to escape.

7   The good-hearted understand what it's like to be poor;
        the hardhearted haven't the faintest idea.

8   A gang of cynics can upset a whole city;
       a group of sages can calm everyone down.

9   A sage trying to work things out with a fool
       gets only scorn and sarcasm for his trouble.

10   Murderers hate honest people;
       moral folks encourage them.

11   A fool lets it all hang out;
       a sage quietly mulls it over.

12   When a leader listens to malicious gossip,
       all the workers get infected with evil.

13   The poor and their abusers have at least something in common:
       they can both *see* — their sight, GOD's gift!

14   Leadership gains authority and respect
       when the voiceless poor are treated fairly.

15   Wise discipline imparts wisdom;
       spoiled adolescents embarrass their parents.

16   When degenerates take charge, crime runs wild,
       but the righteous will eventually observe their collapse.

17   Discipline your children; you'll be glad you did —
       they'll turn out delightful to live with.

18   If people can't see what God is doing,
       they stumble all over themselves;
     But when they attend to what he reveals,
       they are most blessed.

19   It takes more than talk to keep workers in line;
       mere words go in one ear and out the other.

20   Observe the people who always talk before they think —
       even simpletons are better off than they are.

21   If you let people treat you like a doormat,

you'll be quite forgotten in the end.

22   Angry people stir up a lot of discord;
        the intemperate stir up trouble.

23   Pride lands you flat on your face;
        humility prepares you for honors.

24   Befriend an outlaw
        and become an enemy to yourself.
      When the victims cry out,
            you'll be included in their curses
            if you're a coward to their cause in court.

25   The fear of human opinion disables;
        trusting in GOD protects you from that.

26   Everyone tries to get help from the leader,
        but only GOD will give us justice.

27   Good people can't stand the sight of deliberate evil;
        the wicked can't stand the sight of well-chosen goodness.

THE WORDS OF AGUR BEN YAKEH
GOD? WHO NEEDS HIM?

1-2   **30** The skeptic swore, "There is no God!
            No God! — I can do anything I want!
            I'm more animal than human;
      so-called human intelligence escapes me.

3-4   "I flunked 'wisdom.'
        I see no evidence of a holy God.
      Has anyone ever seen Anyone
            climb into Heaven and take charge?
            grab the winds and control them?
            gather the rains in his bucket?
            stake out the ends of the earth?
      Just tell me his name, tell me the names of his sons.
        Come on now — tell me!"

5-6   The believer replied, "Every promise of God proves true;
        he protects everyone who runs to him for help.

So don't second-guess him;
    he might take you to task and show up your lies."

7-9   And then he prayed, "God, I'm asking for two things
    before I die; don't refuse me —
Banish lies from my lips
    and liars from my presence.
Give me enough food to live on,
    neither too much nor too little.
If I'm too full, I might get independent,
    saying, 'God? Who needs him?'
If I'm poor, I might steal
    and dishonor the name of my God."

10   Don't blow the whistle on your fellow workers
    behind their backs;
They'll accuse you of being underhanded,
    and then *you'll* be the guilty one!

11   Don't curse your father
    or fail to bless your mother.

12   Don't imagine yourself to be quite presentable
    when you haven't had a bath in weeks.

13   Don't be stuck-up
    and think you're better than everyone else.

14   Don't be greedy,
    merciless and cruel as wolves,
Tearing into the poor and feasting on them,
    shredding the needy to pieces only to discard them.

15-16 A leech has twin daughters
    named "Gimme" and "Gimme more."

FOUR INSATIABLES

Three things are never satisfied,
    no, there are four that never say, "That's enough, thank you!" —

    hell,
    a barren womb,

a parched land,
a forest fire.

17   An eye that disdains a father
and despises a mother —
that eye will be plucked out by wild vultures
and consumed by young eagles.

FOUR MYSTERIES

18-19   Three things amaze me,
no, four things I'll never understand —

how an eagle flies so high in the sky,
how a snake glides over a rock,
how a ship navigates the ocean,
why adolescents act the way they do.

20   Here's how a prostitute operates:
she has sex with her client,
Takes a bath,
then asks, "Who's next?"

FOUR INTOLERABLES

21-23   Three things are too much for even the earth to bear,
yes, four things shake its foundations —

when the janitor becomes the boss,
when a fool gets rich,
when a whore is voted "woman of the year,"
when a "girlfriend" replaces a faithful wife.

FOUR SMALL WONDERS

24-28   There are four small creatures,
wisest of the wise they are —

ants — frail as they are,
    get plenty of food in for the winter;
marmots — vulnerable as they are,
    manage to arrange for rock-solid homes;
locusts — leaderless insects,

yet they strip the field like an army regiment;
   lizards — easy enough to catch,
     but they sneak past vigilant palace guards.

FOUR DIGNITARIES

29-31 There are three solemn dignitaries,
   four that are impressive in their bearing —

   a lion, king of the beasts, deferring to none;
   a rooster, proud and strutting;
   a billy goat;
   a head of state in stately procession.

32-33 If you're dumb enough to call attention to yourself
   by offending people and making rude gestures,
Don't be surprised if someone bloodies your nose.
   Churned milk turns into butter;
   riled emotions turn into fist fights.

SPEAK OUT FOR JUSTICE

1 **31** The words of King Lemuel,
   the strong advice his mother gave him:

2-3 "Oh, son of mine, what can you be thinking of!
   Child whom I bore! The son I dedicated to God!
Don't dissipate your virility on fortune-hunting women,
   promiscuous women who shipwreck leaders.

4-7 "Leaders can't afford to make fools of themselves,
   gulping wine and swilling beer,
Lest, hung over, they don't know right from wrong,
   and the people who depend on them are hurt.
Use wine and beer only as sedatives,
   to kill the pain and dull the ache
Of the terminally ill,
   for whom life is a living death.

8-9 "Speak up for the people who have no voice,
   for the rights of all the down-and-outers.
Speak out for justice!
   Stand up for the poor and destitute!"

HYMN TO A GOOD WIFE

10-31   A good woman is hard to find,
    and worth far more than diamonds.
Her husband trusts her without reserve,
    and never has reason to regret it.
Never spiteful, she treats him generously
    all her life long.
She shops around for the best yarns and cottons,
    and enjoys knitting and sewing.
She's like a trading ship that sails to faraway places
    and brings back exotic surprises.
She's up before dawn, preparing breakfast
    for her family and organizing her day.
She looks over a field and buys it,
    then, with money she's put aside, plants a garden.
First thing in the morning, she dresses for work,
    rolls up her sleeves, eager to get started.
She senses the worth of her work,
    is in no hurry to call it quits for the day.
She's skilled in the crafts of home and hearth,
    diligent in homemaking.
She's quick to assist anyone in need,
    reaches out to help the poor.
She doesn't worry about her family when it snows;
    their winter clothes are all mended and ready to wear.
She makes her own clothing,
    and dresses in colorful linens and silks.
Her husband is greatly respected
    when he deliberates with the city fathers.
She designs gowns and sells them,
    brings the sweaters she knits to the dress shops.
Her clothes are well-made and elegant,
    and she always faces tomorrow with a smile.
When she speaks she has something worthwhile to say,
    and she always says it kindly.
She keeps an eye on everyone in her household,
    and keeps them all busy and productive.
Her children respect and bless her;
    her husband joins in with words of praise:
"Many women have done wonderful things,
    but you've outclassed them all!"

Charm can mislead and beauty soon fades.
  The woman to be admired and praised
  is the woman who lives in the Fear-of-GOD.
Give her everything she deserves!
  Festoon her life with praises!

Essential Insights

ESSENTIAL INSIGHT 1: *Start with the fundamentals and stick with them.*

ESSENTIAL INSIGHT 2: *Don't look merely to your natural gifts, but focus your energy on marshalling all available resources.*

ESSENTIAL INSIGHT 3: *Decide to put God ahead of everything else in your life.*

ESSENTIAL INSIGHT 4: *Give your heart to God and channel your passions toward personal growth.*

ESSENTIAL INSIGHT 5: *Integrity starts at home. Learn to be a person of your word and stick with your commitments even when you no longer feel like it.*

ESSENTIAL INSIGHT 6: *Patiently wait on God for your success, and He will give you results greater than you could engineer on your own.*

ESSENTIAL INSIGHT 7: *Focus your life on a meaningful mission that inspires your personal discipline and single-mindedness. Don't give in to your unseemly passions.*

ESSENTIAL INSIGHT 8: *Choose to cultivate your inner person, and don't sacrifice your character on the road to success.*

ESSENTIAL INSIGHT 9: *Settle on your life purposes and set out to accomplish them each day.*

ESSENTIAL INSIGHT 10: *Determine that honesty will be a hallmark of your life and pay scrupulous attention to maintaining it at all times, no matter what the cost.*

ESSENTIAL INSIGHT 11: *Work to develop a generous heart toward others and in doing so, give to yourself.*

ESSENTIAL INSIGHT 12: *Learn to harness the power of your tongue and use it to do the greatest possible good.*

ESSENTIAL INSIGHT 13: *Drawing attention to yourself may be good for business, but the simple life is good for your soul.*

ESSENTIAL INSIGHT 14: *Choose your friends carefully.*

ESSENTIAL INSIGHT 15: *Humble yourself before God, and He will lift you up.*

ESSENTIAL INSIGHT 16: *When you make your plans, don't leave God out of the formula. That is the only part that makes any sense.*

ESSENTIAL INSIGHT 17: *Forgiveness is a powerful force in the hands of those who have been wronged.*

ESSENTIAL INSIGHT 18: *Learn to listen and discover life.*

ESSENTIAL INSIGHT 19: *Never give up, no matter how dark the clouds over your head. God has a plan for you that will bring unsurpassed joy to your life.*

ESSENTIAL INSIGHT 20: *Your uncontrolled anger may give you a moment of satisfaction but a lifetime of regret.*

ESSENTIAL INSIGHT 21: *Mere activity is not necessarily a sign of life.*

ESSENTIAL INSIGHT 22: *Weigh your decisions carefully. You can smear a lifetime of accomplishment with doubt in a moment of haste.*

ESSENTIAL INSIGHT 23: *Look beneath the surface — people and circumstances are not always what they appear to be.*

ESSENTIAL INSIGHT 24: *Don't envy the success of the world — it is like a chain of death.*

ESSENTIAL INSIGHT 25: *Always do your best, knowing that God will lift you up and never let you fail.*

ESSENTIAL INSIGHT 26: *As much as is within you, be at peace with all men.*

ESSENTIAL INSIGHT 27: *Give yourself to those you love; trust them to be faithful and accept their input into your life as you would any other act of love.*

ESSENTIAL INSIGHT 28: *Don't put all your eggs in one basket. Sow many acts of value over your lifetime, and you will be amazed at the harvest when you are old.*

ESSENTIAL INSIGHT 29: *An effective leader knows how to manage those under his authority and has the will to do what is right for them.*

ESSENTIAL INSIGHT 30: *Don't let your love of money blind you to what is truly important or valuable. Money is only a tool — it doesn't make you rich.*

ESSENTIAL INSIGHT 31: *Celebrate excellence and discover God's world of opportunity.*

Index of Topics

About the Authors

Eugene H. Peterson

Eugene H. Peterson is a pastor, scholar, writer, and poet. After teaching at a seminary and then giving nearly thirty years to church ministry in the Baltimore area, he created The Message — a vibrant Bible paraphrase that connects with today's readers like no other.

It took Peterson a full ten years to complete. He worked from the original Greek and Hebrew tests to guarantee authenticity. At the same time, his ear was always tuned to the cadence and energy of contemporary English.

Daniel Southern

Daniel Southern loves to observe and learn from the people and experiences God has placed in his life. God has been shaping him through the years as an athlete, traveling for Billy Graham, and leading the American Tract Society. His family, ministry, and local church are paramount among his priorities. Dan's idea of relaxation would be grilling on the barbeque in the backyard with his family close by or enjoying a good conversation with friends over a hot cup of coffee. Although originally from Michigan, Dan now makes his home in Texas.

THE BEST MESSAGE ON EARTH JUST GOT BETTER.